1

# Tear Down the Silos
## And
## Pitch a Tent

Tom Couser

Tear Down the Silos and Pitch a Tent


Copyright, 2021 by Tom Couser




In writing this book Tom used the New International Version (NIV), Thompson Chain-Reference Bible, co-published by B. B. Kirkbride Co. and The Zondervan Corporation.

# Advanced Praise for

# Tear Down the Silos and Pitch a Tent

We all know that times are changing. Let's be honest, we're not ready for it and we're not sure where to start. If you're a pastor or a church leader, Tom gives words to what you're thinking and feeling and helps you get the conversation started. Thank you, Tom, for giving us the courage to trust Jesus, the Lord of the Church, who calls us to, "Tear down the silo and pitch a tent."

Micah Miller

Senior Pastor of Prince of Peace Lutheran Church in Carrollton, Texas

* * * *

Tom's love for Jesus' and His people permeates his message to us in this book. He invites intentional consideration for our spiritual legacy and the future of those God works to redeem through His Church.  In these pages, Tom models a contemplative life to find God's presence in ourselves, our communities, and our efforts to reach the souls God loves.  Tom sees how God's Truth has often been muffled by our traditions and practices.  In the process, we serve ourselves and ignore the wandering souls near us. But we do not have to continue along this path.

God's Church will never die, so our expressions of faith with a worshipping, equipping community can embrace these days of confused philosophies.  We can be confidant the Holy Spirit will lead us in God's ultimate plan.  We have the true legacy in Christ to share with the world.  "The thief comes only to kill and destroy; I have come that they may have life, and have it to the full," Jesus, John 10:10, ESV. We know God has this heart for all people and it is ours to share with joy! Tom invites us to have the full life he has embraced and to give it away in new meaningful ways for the souls God is redeeming around us.

Dave Rahberg, Retired DCE

* * * *

My acquaintance with the author goes back to our days serving churches in the Dallas Metro area.  As Directors of Christian Education we would meet Monday mornings at 6:30am to read some scripture, "break some bread" (a bagel) and pray for each other as we sought the "new thing" God was doing in our respective ministries.  We were very much steeped in the parish model, but knew there was something else that we needed to explore. The need to raise up a new generation of missionaries led me to another form of ministry, the short-term mission trip. For many years this became a way to teach youth to reach beyond their "silo" and go into all the world with the light of Christ.  Tom Couser's recounting of His ministry journey and the recognition that even when we get sidetracked and siloed, reminds us that God is still Lord and His Kingdom will never disappear.  As part of the Legacy church referenced in Chapter 3, it has been my privilege to watch God take a "remnant" of Christendom and break free of its silo, guiding it to be a missional movement in the community.  I heartily encourage you to "Tear down Your Silo and Pitch Your Tent" in the nearest hurting community in your town or city or suburb where God leads.

Ron Scherch has served as a parish DCE, Exe. Director of CAN-DO Missions. and Director of Recruitment for LCMS World Mission

* * * *

Tom Couser has presented a stimulating examination of the manner in which we need to respond as Abraham did, in LISTENING to what God is telling us, MOVING into the unknown and pitching our tent, and finally BUILDING an Altar to the Lord to center our outreach to people. The decline of our churches is a reality. How are we to respond? Tom offers a very personal approach with explanations and options as our churches face the challenges of our day; NOT to issues of doctrine and Biblical Truths but to issues of style, methodology and awareness. Our daily ministry must be in the midst of the lost and broken.

Dr. Gerald C. Brunworth is a retired church educator and former headmaster at Lutheran High School of Dallas

# Introduction

On two levels, this is the book I did not want to write. For starters, writing a book is a lot of work. I have been down this road before and was not sure I wanted to invest the time and energy into another project. Secondly, I am an admitted affirmation addict and I knew from the start many of the things I wanted to say would make some people uncomfortable, perhaps even angry. When you suggest that mainline denominations might be going away and that those magnificent sanctuaries we have built might be devalued in the future, you can almost expect some criticism.

Yet, even the casual observer can recognize that the landscape in America is changing when it comes to traditional, mainline Christianity. As I drive around north Dallas, I see countless once successful churches now sitting vacant. Most existing congregations have plateaued or are in decline. Mega Churches, on the other hand, seem to be flourishing. These were the realities I was grappling with. My previous research had provided me some insights into the how and why. As a result, I had the outline for a book that would tackle many of the issues. I just had no desire to follow through.

It was while I was recovering from hip replacement surgery in August,2019 that I had a "come to Jesus" moment. One of the major struggles during recovery was that I was forced to sleep flat on my back. That was a challenge for a long-established "side-sleeper." That reality, coupled with the pain-medication led to some pretty bizarre dreams. In the midst of that one night, God placed a thought in my head: Tear Down the Silos and Pitch a Tent. It took a while but I finally connected-the-dots, God had given me a title for the project I had been trying to avoid.  It seemed like the "heavenly memo" was clear.  God wanted me to write another book.

After developing the outline, I set out to bounce the ideas off some good pastor friends who I respected.  I started with my good friend Micah Miller.  Micah is senior pastor at Prince of Peace Lutheran Church in Carrollton, Texas.  Barb and I are members a Prince of Peace and I wanted to make sure Micah was on-board with what I was going to say.  He became a more trusted friend throughout the process and offered me real guidance after reading the initial manuscript.

I also had lunch with my long-time friend, Dr. John Messmann who is senior pastor of St. Paul Lutheran Church in Fort Worth.  John Messmann confirmed many of my observations.  He also suggested I read the book Rising Tides, by Neil Cole which further stimulated me to follow through on the project.

For sixteen years Barb and I were members of Crown of Life Lutheran Church in Colleyville, Texas, where Barb served as director of music.  Crown of Life has a very distinctive missional mindset.  I spent time visiting with pastors, Dave Jung, Ben Scheck and Martin Richardson.  One of the more unique ministries to grow out of Crown of Life was The Edge Coffee House in Lake Worth, Texas.  I also had a long conversation with Pastor Steve Sandfort about that ministry.

For over twenty years our son Peter was on staff at St. Paul Lutheran Church in Fort Worth.  During the last half of that time, he served as lead pastor at their satellite campus, The Summit in Aledo.  During the early stages of writing this book Peter accepted one of the most unique pastoral calls I am aware of.  The call was to jointly serve First Lutheran Church and Concordia Preparatory School in Towson, Maryland.  First Lutheran had voted to close and was now partnering with Concordia Prep to plant a new worship community.   I have had numerous conversations with both Peter and Ron Scherch, a member of the joint-ministry planning team.

Once the manuscript was written I turned it over to a couple of trusted acquaintances for feedback.  I owe a debt of gratitude to Tim Hetzner, President of Lutheran Church Charities and Dr. Gerald Brunworth, a retired Lutheran educator and long-time member of the Texas District-LCMS board of directors for their feedback.  I also value the comments from my good friend Dave Rahberg.

I also am grateful for the work of Ann Mock who took on the job of editing the original manuscript.

Lastly, I am thankful for my son Mark for reading the manuscript and then writing the foreword.  Mark serves as Pastor of Tree of Life Lutheran Church in Garland, Texas.

I pray you will find the book both a challenging and helpful read.  My desire is to help your church confront the changes that lie ahead and to continually follow the Great Commission to "go and make disciples."


Tom Couser

# Foreword

Can I be honest? I really wish this book didn't have to be written. As a lifelong member of a declining church body (the Lutheran Church-Missouri Synod) and as a parish pastor in that denomination, there were chunks of this book that were hard to swallow. But this is a book that every believer needs to read and take to heart!

I have been a part of some thriving ministries and have seen firsthand the powerful transformation that happens when we live out our Christian faith outside of the four walls of the church. I have been on the staff at an established church that tried to think outside the box and eventually chose to be more conventional. I fear that church may die in the next 5-10 years. Just recently, I heard of a 75-year-old congregation that used to be thriving but during the pandemic their in-person attendance dwindled and they ran out of money. They have closed and are selling their building. This is a stark reality for many of our local congregations if we do not change.

I am grateful for the sincere, thoughtful and biblical approach that the writer (who just happens to be my Dad) takes in approaching these exciting and yet unparalleled times as the body of Christ.

I plan on using this book with my church leadership as we wrestle as a 160-person congregation that is getting older and needs to grow to continue to disciple the saved and to reach the lost with the gospel of Jesus Christ.

As I write these words, we are only a week removed from a terrible event in modern U.S. history. On January 6, 2021 a mob of people tried to seize the U.S. capitol as they tried to harm public servants who were performing their civic duty. This event reminded me that our government and our country is not "the hope of the world", Jesus is! It's time for us as the body of Christ, God's kingdom people on earth, to get back to the Great Commission and the way that the early church lived out their faith in the Book of Acts.


One last thing, it is an honor to be asked to write the foreword for this book. I have to say that I am so proud to be called the son of the author, Tom Couser. My Dad not only "talks a good game", he lives it out day to day. I recently witnessed this on a trip that my Dad and I made to Michigan to pay our respects to my Dad's uncle and my godfather, Donald Ulbrich. We were driving through Indianapolis in rush hour traffic and my Dad was behind the wheel. Up ahead of us we saw a dust cloud pop up suddenly on the side of the road. As we drove closer, we saw a car that had rolled off the highway and was sitting on its side. My Dad immediately pulled the car over and before I could even say anything, my 74-year-old father ran out of the car and headed straight for our distressed neighbor. I knew what my Dad was doing. He was checking on them to make sure they were okay and then he was praying with them in the name of Jesus. I called 9-1-1 and reported the accident as my Dad ran to where help was needed. The lady was ok and the paramedics were on the scene in a few minutes. This is a metaphor as well for this book and for our lives in Christ. There are people around us in crisis, in desperate need for help. They need someone to love them and to step into their chaos with the grace and hope of Jesus. We are God's church. Let's get to work and pitch some tents and move with the Holy Spirit to see Christ's church set a flame again like it was in the 1st century!

Mark T. Couser, Pastor

Tree of Life Lutheran Church

Garland, TX 75043

# CHAPTER 1

## Tents and Silos

"From there he moved to the hill country on the east of
Bethel,

And pitched his tent, with Bethel on the west and Ai on
the east.

And there he built an altar to the Lord and called upon
the name of the Lord."

Genesis 12:8

Abram had been on quite a journey.  He had traveled
from Ur of the Chaldeans to Haran and eventually to
Canaan.  The Lord had directed Abram, "Go from your
country and your father's house to the land I will show
you." (Genesis 12:1) There was a promise, "I will make
you a great nation" and "in you all the families of the
earth shall be blessed."  (Genesis 12:2-3)

There were challenges still ahead when they arrived in
Canaan.  For one thing, the land was already occupied.
Still the Lord's promise was loud and clear, "To your
offspring I will give this land." (Genesis 12:7) Abram's
response was spontaneous; he pitched a tent and built an
altar.

It was a pattern we saw repeated in the life of Abram.  In
a sense, Abram was on a never-ending excursion.  His
initial stay in Canaan was brief.  A drought and a famine
caused Abram to travel to Egypt.  On return, he and his
nephew, Lot, discovered the land was not big enough for
both of them and their families.  The decision was made
to separate.  Lot chose the Jordan Valley.  Abram settled

in the must less fertile plains of Canaan.  Again, God
restated His promise, "I will give you this land" and yes
"you will have more offspring than you can count."
(Genesis 13:14-15)   As was his pattern, Abram pitched a
tent and "built an altar to the Lord."

Abram's journey is condensed into two chapters of
Genesis.  In actuality, it took years, perhaps even
decades.  It was a daunting task to move a large family
with all their possessions and livestock over 500 miles,
not including the side trip to Egypt.  Still, Abram made
the trip because he heard clearly from God that he was
part of a bigger plan.

> 1. God spoke.
>
> 2. Abram Listened.
>
> 3. Abram moved and pitched a tent.
>
> 4. Abram built an altar.

In the process, we can learn three basic principles: 1) We
need to listen to God's command and take them
seriously. 2) We need to move into the unknown and
pitch our tents there.  3) Once there, we are to build an
altar and worship God.

**Worshipping in a Tent**

Back in the 70's, I was teaching a 5th grade weekday
school class.  The curriculum had a lesson on Old
Testament worship titled God's Mobile Home. Yes,
during their wilderness wanderings the Children of Israel
worshipped in a tent.  God gave Moses the instructions
for a sanctuary in the Book of Exodus (Exodus 25:8).
When we hear it was called the tabernacle, we somehow

picture a magnificent building.  While it was indeed constructed of the finest materials, it was very much a moveable structure that could be disassembled and moved as needed.

The tabernacle was more than just a place of worship.  In the Old Testament, it was frequently called the "tent of meetings," indicating that it was the place Moses went to encounter God.   Unlike the pile of stones that served Abram as an altar, there was a sense of intimacy within the tabernacle.  God was indeed in the midst of His people and they could meet Him where they lived

We read of one such meeting in Exodus 33.  God was frustrated with the stubborn attitude of the "stiff-necked" people.  Moses went to meet God outside of the camp where the tabernacle was located.  It is noted that Abram went to the "tent of meetings" where he spoke with the Lord, "face-to-face as a man speaks with his friends." (Exodus 33:11)   The Old Testament tabernacle was not just a place for worship but also a place to encounter God in an intimate way.

The tabernacle concept is one that contemporary Christians should consider as an option.  Consider how revolutionary it would be to have a "tent of meeting" in every neighborhood.  I would be a place where God's people could gather and meet him face-to-face as a friend.  It would not only bring worship into the midst of the people, but make it easier to invite friends and neighbors to come and meet God as well.

One of my favorite television shows of all time is MASH. MASH is an acronym for Mobile Army Surgical Hospital.  The unit really was a cluster of tents that could be disassembled and moved to a new location, always moving to where the action was.  In many ways, the church of the future needs to be more like a MASH unit than a tabernacle.  The old parish model was "if we build it, they will come."  Ministry happened in and around the church.  A MASH Unit church is mobile and out in the community.  It can easily be taken down and moved to another spot as the needs change.

Do we still need a more central location where the disciples can gather to be trained and equipped?  Definitely! Worship and celebration happen in those times when the people of God gather around the Word and the Sacrament.  However, the real ministry happens in the community around the area where those portable worship centers/tabernacles are located.  Those are the "tents of meeting" where God comes face-to-face with His people.


## Silos

During the 70's and 80's, our family was living in the Chicago area.  Since my wife's parents lived in St. Louis, we often found ourselves traveling there.  In the early years, that meant traveling on old Route 66.  The Illinois Central Railroad mainline ran parallel to the highway much of time.  That part of Illinois is perfectly flat, so you can look across miles and miles of farmland.  They grow an abundance of wheat, corn and soy beans in Illinois.  There were many small towns along the highway: Dwight, Pontiac, Lincoln and Litchfield to name a few.  Each town had a railroad siding where you would find a grain elevator with a series of at least three or more grain silos.  You would always need at least three silos in Illinois, because you could not mix the grain.  Some silos held corn, others soy beans and still others wheat.

If I looked past the grain elevator into the town, I would see other silos.  They were not cylindrical like the grain silos, rather they were usually brick structures that featured tall spires on the top.  Some of those silos held Catholics, others held Lutherans or Methodist.  You need different kinds of religious silos to hold the different kinds of Christians, because in small town America, the different denominations do not mix.  Each of the churches/silos holds a different kind of Christian.  Each of them has unique traditions and doctrines and the people within those silos all tend to share them.  There was not a lot of religious cross-pollinating in small town America.

For decades, the same pattern existed in urban America.  Different denominations could exist within the same neighborhood, but they typically did not mix well.  Each existed within its own silo.  To gain entry you had to, in a sense, pass a test.  You had to share the same faith traditions. In a sense, even kind of look and think alike.  Lutherans would not be caught dead at bingo night at the Catholic parish and you definitely would not find a Baptist attending Beer and Brat night in the Lutheran fellowship hall.

Silo ministry served us well for decades.  Sometime in the early 70's, winds of change blew through America.  The old way of doing ministry within the silo was less effective.  The Baby Boomers, born post World War II, were the first to break the mold.  There was less respect for the traditions within a particular silo.  Suddenly, Lutherans were marrying Methodists and Baptists were marrying Presbyterians.  The lines between the denominations became blurred.  In many ways, the non-denominational mega churches were born out of the desire for young families to find a middle ground.


**More Silos**

There are more than just denominational silos.  I became very much aware of that early in my ministry.  My office was located in the youth center that was part of a much larger building, housing the parish school, gym and fellowship center.  Located within the structure were four distinct kitchens, all fully equipped with the latest appliances.  Because of state health restrictions, the parish school had its own kitchen.  I could live with that.

What always troubled me was the lines demarcation between the other three.  The men's club shared a kitchen with the Boys Scouts.  The Scouts also stored much of their camping gear in a closet off that kitchen.  For that reason, it was always locked.  I was fortunate in that several of the scouts were involved in my youth ministry.  They knew where a key was hidden.  On occasion, I would go in to borrow items; always careful to put them back.

The youth ministry team always used what was referred to as the "fellowship kitchen."  It was the general facility available to any groups using the building.  It contained a hodge-podge of cooking utensils and pots and pans.  The custodial staff usually kept it reasonably clean.

The most hallowed area in the whole building was "The Guild Kitchen."  It was totally off limits to anyone except a sacred few.  It was always locked and secured like a fortress.  The strange thing was; when the Women's Guild met, they held their meetings in the fellowship hall and used the fellowship kitchen.  The "Guild Kitchen," with its fine china and polished silverware, was only used on rare occasions, like a pastoral conference or the annual Christmas Bazaar.

The above example points out how traditional parish ministry can easily lead to 'silos."  It can simply become a competition for space, active participants and a slice of the budget.  The silos are defined by age, gender, interest or specific need.  Instead of working together to build up the body of Christ, they can become ministries in and of themselves.

* * * *

Today, we are seeing the end result of silo stye ministry. Most local denominational churches are in decline, or at best reached a plateau.  It is time to admit the reality; we need to tear down the existing silos and begin to pitch more tents.  We need to think outside the box, that is the typical church, and seek new ways of doing ministry.  The church of the future must be more mobile and open to doing ministry in the midst of the lost and broken.  It must also do so across racial and ethnic lines.

That is what this book is all about.  We will be looking at the challenges Christians in America will need to explore for the future of the church... maybe even your church. Many changes lie ahead.  We need to explore the role of mainline denominations.  Many of the current ways we do ministry no longer works.  We are facing times when there will be fewer pastors and full-time ministry professionals.

It is time to tear down the silos and begin to pitch some tents!

# CHAPTER 2

## Understanding My Context

All of us have experiences that shape who we are. The town and environment we grew up in is part of our history. Our ethnic heritage and family are a big part of who we are. Our education influences us. So does our experience when it comes to faith and the practices thereof. Our family and the mentors we have along the way all play a role in who we are today. I think it is important that you understand my context and the experiences that have molded my life. All those elements have brought me to this point in my life and have impacted my opinions and perspectives.

I graduated from Lutheran High School East in Harper Woods, Michigan in 1964. There were ninety-seven of us in that graduating class. Our commencement celebration was held jointly with our sister school, Lutheran High School West, at the Ford Auditorium in downtown Detroit. Like the rest of my classmates, I was a member of a Lutheran Church in the Detroit area.

I grew up on the eastside of Detroit. Our community was like others in the Motor City. Every neighborhood had a Lutheran Church that served the families, often within walking distance. In our case, there were two Lutheran Church Missouri Synod (LCMS) churches, Peace on East Warren and Bethany (locate less than a mile away) on East Outer Drive. Peace and Bethany operated thriving parish schools and they were bitter rivals. Somehow those students became classmates at Lutheran High East, along with kids from similar schools like East Bethlehem and St. Peter in East Detroit.

I was a bit of an oddity at Lutheran East. My parents
were members of St. James Lutheran in suburban Grosse
Pointe. St James did not operate a parish school. As a
result, I attended Finney, a public school, which was just a
short two block walk from our house. The plan was
always for me to attend Lutheran East once I was ready
for high school. By the time we graduated from high
school we had all blended together but the directory in
the back of the school yearbook listed the name of our
home Lutheran Church. This proving, Lutheran High
School East was 100% "certified Lutheran."

Rev. George Kurz was the only pastor I knew growing up.
He spent his entire ministry at St. James Lutheran
Church. He had been called to start a new church in the
growing suburb. They had their first worship in the local
library, but quickly moved to a local movie theater, The
Punch and Judy. That is where I was baptized. My dad
used to joke that I was baptized "in the punch." Shortly
after my baptism, the church moved to its new sanctuary
on McMillan Road.

My parents were very involved at St. James. My dad
served as Sunday school superintendent for ten years.
During that time, our family was usually the first to arrive
on Sunday morning and often the last to leave. Our
family car was a green 1953 Willys. It was usually parked
in the first spot in the parking lot, signaling that the doors
were open. My parents were in the senior choir that sang
every Sunday morning at the 11:00a.m. service. My
siblings and I usually sat in the pew with my grandmother.
A roll of Lifesavers came out of her purse during the

sermon.  Pastor Kurz's sermons were usually good for three Lifesavers.


St. James Lutheran Church was a busy place in the fifties and the sixties.  The building was bursting at the seams with kids.  There were twenty-five in my confirmation class in 1959.  That was typical.  The two Sunday morning worship services were packed.  I recall over fifty of us singing in the children's choir, led by our organist, Carl Munzel.  During my junior year in high school, I was asked to join the bass section of the senior choir.


Some lessons learned at St. James have stayed with me.  I recall one Lenten season, in particular, during my high school years.  The period before Easter was a stressful time for the choir.  In addition to singing every Sunday, we sang at the Wednesday night Lenten Services as well, often performing a full Lenten cantata for one of those services.  In this case, the grind had taken its toll and the rehearsal was not going well.  We were struggling to learn the anthem for Easter.  Carl Munzel was not a big man and he walked with a distinct limp, the result of polio as a child.  On this evening, he had enough. He rose from the piano bench and sternly addressed the choir.  "You don't get it," he shouted! "If this was Christmas music, we would not have this problem because Christmas is about a baby.  If the baby Jesus stayed in a manger, we would have nothing to celebrate.  This is Easter and He rose from the dead.  We are Easter people," he exclaimed!


* * * *

I graduated from Concordia Teachers College in River Forest, Illinois (now Concordia University-Chicago) in the spring of 1969 and entered full-time ministry shortly thereafter.  My training was in education, but my area of specialty was youth ministry.  I was eventually certified as a director of Christian education (DCE).  I served four different Lutheran Churches and then spent my last eleven years as a school counselor at Lutheran High School of Dallas.  I retired in 2007 and began the writing ministry I carry on till this day.

I met my future wife, Barbara Brown, at Concordia.  She was also an education major but in addition, was taking organ lessons in preparation for a career in music ministry.  Barb ended up teaching in a Lutheran School for three years and eventually moved into positions of organist and music director at congregations where we served.

All the churches we served followed the same parish model I grew up with.

Trinity Lutheran Church in Cape Girardeau, Missouri was our first call.  We had graduated Memorial Day Weekend, were married on June 14th and arrived at our first assignment on July 1st.  Talk about a whirlwind month!  My new bride, Barb, taught second grade in the parish school and I was youth director.  There were a lot of youth to direct in those days.  Trinity had over 2,500 members and over 200 of them were high school teens. It got pretty crazy in the youth room.  We did raise some eyebrows when we started singing to guitar music, and even more when we had the first dance in the school basement.

The youth group at Trinity was still called The Walther League, the traditional name for an LCMS youth group. In addition to Sunday morning Bible class, the Trinity Walther League met every Sunday night. On Monday night, we had a youth discussion group, usually tackling current issues. The Vietnam War was still raging and "peace and love" were the hot topics, but so were drugs and sexuality. I walked a fine-line when it came to the war issue. Our pastor, Oscar Gerken, often wore a tie that featured red, white and blue. The congregational members were pretty conservative and few questioned the war effort. I raised a few eyebrows by wearing a button with a "peace symbol."

We moved from Missouri to the Chicago area in 1972. My call was to serve as director of Christian education (DCE) at Immanuel Lutheran Church in Downers Grove. In many ways, Immanuel was a prototypical church for that era. The Lutheran Church Missouri Synod was in its "hay days". Immanuel, under the leadership of Pastor William C. Huener, was flourishing. With almost 1,000 adult members, Immanuel was a "beehive" of activity. We had a growing Sunday school and each summer, we would host a two-week Vacation Bible School that one year attracted over 500 kids from the community. I stayed busy administrating all the parish and education youth ministry programs. My job description actually had the term "from womb to tomb" in it.

In 1980, we made the move from Downers Grove to the northwest suburb of West Dundee. I had accepted the call to be DCE at Bethlehem Lutheran Church. In many ways, Bethlehem was similar to my previous position. I was an education generalist, overseeing children's, youth and adult education ministries. I also assisted in worship, even preaching once or twice a month. It was during my time in Dundee that I began to sense the winds of change within the church. It was more difficult to get the teens engaged in ministry and over-all there was less of a commitment to Christian education on the part of the parents.

We moved to Dallas in the summer of 1988 when I accepted a call to be director of youth and young adult ministry at Holy Cross Lutheran Church. I spent seven years at Holy Cross. I saw many changes during those years but probably none greater than the decline in Sunday school attendance and a drop in participation in youth ministry. Not only were the numbers down but it was harder to get people to volunteer. Still the pressure from congregational leaders was on. The expectation was they would see the same results they always had. I felt some guilt as well because I did not see the same level of participation and commitment I has seen in the past. It is only now that I realize I was witnessing the end of the parish ministry model.

* * * *

My first car was a 1956 Plymouth that I bought in August of 1964. I had graduated from high school and was going to trade school and working a part-time job. I needed basic transportation. Like many Chrysler products in those years, it was fast but severely lacking in body integrity. My friends called it a "Flintstone car" because there was a hole in the floor in the backseat and you could literally put your feet through it. Fortunately, I found a piece of sheet metal in the garage that was just the right size to cover the gap. That problem was easy. Solving the issue with the doors was a different matter. The only fully functioning door was on the front passenger's side. The door on the driver's side in front did not open at all. The rear doors only opened from the outside. It did present an issue for Friday night dates.

In the spring of 1965, my Uncle Don offered to sell me his 1959 Chevy. He was buying a new car and rather than trade it in he had pity on me. I sold the Plymouth for $25 and stepped up to the luxury of a car that was not only dependable but had four functioning doors. I was in heaven.

As great as that 1959 Chevy was, it is nothing compared to the car I drive today. It had no power steering or power brakes. The only air conditioning was two vents under the dashboard on either side of the car. All it had was an AM Radio. No FM or Satellite radio like my current Chrysler. By the way, my current vehicle has 180,000 miles on it and still runs just fine, thank you! The engine of that 1959 Chevy needed to be rebuilt at 60,000 miles.

What is the point? Think about how much our cars have changed over the last fifty years. The same could be said for our phones, televisions and so many other conveniences we enjoy. The high definition, flat screen television I watch is quite a step up from the heavy square box filled with tubes that offered only black and white images. No way am I going back to the good old days of rotary phones and having to heat water on the stove. Yes, no microwave ovens in those days!

The point is, it is a different world.  Unfortunately, many churches still operate with the old model.  Granted, we have moved forward when it comes to media and technology, but most churches use the same "parish model" for ministry.  You plant a church in a neighborhood, bring in a pastor and expect people to come.  To make things attractive, you add a nursery and Sunday school.  You offer an active youth ministry program and have Bible studies for the adults.  There is a men's ministry and women's guild.  Active churches might still have a choir and full music ministry.  That is the way the Christian church has operated for centuries, but... . . .  it is no longer working.


For decades, many Protestants saw the same cycle repeat itself.  Children were baptized and three or four years later started Sunday school.  In the case of many Lutheran congregations, the children even attended a parish school where religion was taught on a daily basis and they regularly attended chapel. In most cases, children went through some kind of instruction beginning in 7th grade.  Confirmation class, as it was called, led to becoming adult members.  After confirmation, they moved into the church youth group.  Often, they disappeared for a few years while they went off to college and started their careers.  No worry: when it was time to be married, they came back to church.  A few years later, they came back to have their children baptized and the cycle began again.  What happens when they no longer come back?  That is the dilemma we face today.


* * * *

I have shared all the previous information so that you understand the context that I am coming from.  My best guess is that many of you reading this book share a similar experience.  If you grew up in the church, you probably have parallel memories.  You went to Sunday school and in the summer, you went to Vacation Bible School.  Sometimes you even went with friends to experience VBS at their church, where somehow the Kool-Aid and cookies tasted the same even though they sang songs that were a little different.  You probably were part of a church youth group and maybe even met your spouse in that environment.

Like many of you, I cherish the memories of the church of the past, but the reality is many of those recollections have become obstacles.  We cling to the old tried and true while the waves of change rage around us.  We gather Sunday after Sunday, worshipping in the same place as we watch the numbers dwindle.  We visit with old friends around the coffee pot after church and wonder why people don't visit us anymore.  As we wander down the hallway of the education wing to Bible class, we wonder why the classrooms are empty.

While our past experiences have everything to do with how we got to this moment in our lives, they have nothing to do with the future.  What happens when...

- the culture shifts, and the church is no longer the center of people's lives like it was in the past.

- The model for the way we do ministry changes, the old methods no longer produce the results we expect.

- The rules change, and the government no longer views the church in the same way?

All of the above are not only possible but have become part of our current reality.  In many ways the 2020 pandemic has been a wake-up call.  The church, like the rest of society, has been forced to change.  Pastors and others church professionals have had to find new and creative ways to do ministry.  I even hear folks talk about "getting back to normal."  For me, I sense that means going back to the way things were.  The truth is, things have not been that way for a long time.  The decline in church membership and attendance has been happening for decades.  The progression has been so gradual than many folks sitting in the pew have not even noticed.

Reality Check: The church after the pandemic is going to look vastly different.  We really have no choice.

The good news is that there is still time.  God's love is the same.  The promise that we have in Jesus Christ is still the only hope for a broken world!  We are still called to be the hands, feet, and voice of Jesus in that world.

The recognition of the need to change is the first step.

# CHAPTER 3

## Churches in America Today

The Christian Church is very much alive in the United States! Granted, most mainline denominations are experiencing a decline but overall a majority of Americans self-identify as Christian and a good portion of these folks practice their faith regularly.  Each year, The Barna Group publishes a report on the status of Christianity in America.  According to the 2019 Barna research, 75% of U.S. adults self-identify as Christian.  On the downside, the numbers drop by generation with Elders (over 65) leading the way with 83% claiming to be Christian.  The percentages drop dramatically from there: 80% of Boomers, 73% of Gen Xers and 64% of Millennials.  When it comes to practicing the Christian faith, the numbers were not as encouraging.  Almost four in 10 Elders (37%) practice their faith by attending a worship service regularly.  Again, it is trending down from Boomers (30%) to Gen Xers (26%) and Millennials (22%). [1]

So where are all the Christians and where are they worshipping?  From my perspective, most Christian worship communities fall into one of three groups: mega churches, cornerstone churches, and terminal churches.  There is an emerging fourth group: legacy churches that

---

[1] Barna.org

give me the greatest hope for the future, but more on that
later.


## Mega Churches

My first experience with a mega church came in the mid-
eighties. I was serving in a Lutheran Church in West
Dundee, a northwest suburb of Chicago. Willow Creek
Community Church was located in nearby Barrington
Hills. I was previously aware of Willow Creek because I
had crossed paths with their founding pastor, Bill Hybels.
Bill started his ministry as a youth pastor. He and I
attended some of the same training events. Willow
Creek began as a youth-focused ministry at the Willow
Creek Movie Theater in Palatine, Illinois. Over time, the
church grew and purchased the property in Barrington
Hills for their campus.

The way members of the local ministry alliance first
talked about Willow Creek you would have thought Bill
Hybels was the antichrist. There were all kinds of
alarmed accusations of sheep stealing. It was not just the
clergy who were concerned. Our congregational leaders
were also irritated when we started to have some folks
drift toward Willow Creek. I know that some of our
teens were attending the Wednesday night Son City youth
ministry. My experience is that what goes around comes
around. In time, we gained some former Willow Creek
members who were looking for a more intimate,
relational experience.

* * * *

The Hartford Institute for Religion Research defines a
mega church as any Protestant Christian church having
2,000 or more people in average weekend attendance.[2]

31

On one weekend in November 2015, around one in ten Protestant churchgoers in the U.S., or about 5 million people, attended service in a mega church. One such church, Lakewood Church in Houston, averages over 45,000 worshippers each Sunday. Under the leadership of Joel Osteen, they gather in an arena that was once used by the NBA Houston Rockets. Another renowned mega church is Saddleback Church in California, which is led by Rick Warren.

My wife and I are members of Prince of Peace Lutheran Church in Carrollton, Texas. Within a half a mile of our church is Prestonwood Baptist Church. The campus includes a 7,000-seat worship center, and a school offering Pre-Kindergarten through Grade 12, including athletic fields. It is one of the largest churches in America, with a membership of over 45,000 and a weekly attendance of around 17,000. The Plano campus covers an area of 140 acres. They have a second campus in Prosper, Texas.

Mega Churches are not just a North American phenomenon. Five of the ten largest Protestant churches are in South Korea.[3] As of 2007, the current largest mega church in the world is South Korea's Yoido Full Gospel Church, an Assemblies of God church, with more than 830,000 members.

In 1986 I received an insight into what makes Mega Churches attractive when I sat down with Judson Poling who at that time was director of pastoral ministries at Willow Creek. I was doing an interview for Insights into

Christian Education, a publication I was involved with at the time. Judson Poling spoke of how intentional Willow Creek was at marketing their ministry toward men. "If we are serious about building families, how are we going to reach men? Most men are not attracted to the typical church service," he stated. "Our Sunday morning experience is designed to reach the 30-35 year old male," he continued. "If we reach them, we will get their wife and kids," he concluded.

While the culture has changed somewhat from the 80's, the same approach makes Mega Churches attractive today. In our current climate, many young people are delaying marriage until they are in their thirties. When and if, they start a family, it will be even later. Still Millennials and Gen Z's value relationships. They want to network with others their age. The challenge for the church comes in touching the lives of these folks. Mega churches, with their many entry points, are better equipped to do that. They offer health clubs, coffee bars and recovery groups, all ways to touch the lives of people. Many of these touch points are especially attractive to young men. If you can attract young men, the young women will follow. Decades ago, the church youth and young adult groups provided a way for a couple to connect, date and eventually marry. Today it is Mega Churches playing that role. I am convinced that is what drives much of their success.

**Cornerstone Churches**

Cornerstone Churches are just that: foundations in their community. Normally these churches are connected to a mainline denomination.  Typically, these churches average two hundred or more in worship every week. This makes them more sustainable.  As smaller congregations in the same denomination shrink in size, these churches will experience some growth as members leave the declining worship communities.

There are other factors that make these worship communities more viable.

1)	They are cross generational.  Unlike churches that have separate ministries for children, youth, young adults, these churches seek to establish a community feeling where people of all ages gather to celebrate. While equipping parents is a high priority, so is encouraging older adults to share the heritage of faith.

2)	They engage with the community.  These churches seek ways to reach out and minister to those around them.  They are supportive of community ministries like the local food pantry.  They partner with local public schools to support children from low-income families and to encourage the teachers and staff. They also make their facilities available to community groups.

3)	They seek to meet the worship needs of a variety of people by offering multiple styles of worship.  They also attempt to reach those whose schedule does not allow them to worship on Sunday morning, by offering alternative worship times.

4)	They encourage a missional lifestyle.  They are intentional in equipping members to reach out to those around them who do not know the saving grace of Jesus Christ.  They also recognize the reality that the lost probably are not going to come to them.  Hence, they work to establish smaller worship communities in local neighborhoods or apartment complexes.

## Terminal Churches

Thom Rainer is the former CEO and President of Lifeway Christian Resources. He continues to serve the church as a writer and a consultant. In the February 27, 2020 edition of his Rainer on Leadership, Thom Rainer stated "More than 10% of churches in North America are at risk of closing."[4] Thom Rainer is not the first to make such a prediction. In their 2009 book Legacy Churches, Stephen Gray and Franklin Drumond forecast that by 2030 50% of the churches of the Southern Baptist Convention, one of the largest denominations in the world, will be on a course to close. [5]

Terminal churches are located in a variety of settings. Many are in small towns and rural areas. These churches have fallen victim to the shift away from an agrarian society to an urban one. Others are located in major cities where the community has changed or even declined economically. We can even find terminal churches in once fast-growing suburbs.

If we are looking for a common theme that links many of these dying worship communities together it can be found in two common threads. They are more focused on holding onto traditions, including the attachment to a

---

4 Thom S. Rainer, Growing Healthy Church, 2-27-20
5 Legacy Churches, Stephen Gray and Franklin Drumond, Smart Church Resources, 2009, Pg. 32

building, than reaching the lost Secondly, they have failed to adjust to change both in terms of culture and community. These two factors have combined to turn a once fertile field into a dry desert.

There are some additional factors that have changed many local churches from being vibrant and alive to terminally ill.

The exit of the Builder generation. The Builder generation has kept many churches alive, even if the congregations are on life support. This generation, born before 1946, is fiercely loyal to institutions, including local churches. They stuck with congregations in good and bad times. By 2015, there were only 28 million Builders left. Another 13,000 Builders die every week. This loyal generation is fewer in number and will soon be no more!

Migration from rural areas and small towns to the cities. In 1790, only 5% of Americans lived in cities. By the 1960s, the percentage of Americans in cities skyrocketed to 65%. Today over 80% of Americans are city dwellers. Rural and small-town churches held on tenaciously to their members for over two centuries. The population base for those tenacious churches has dwindled dramatically.

People are quicker to transfer from one church to another. Those who are transferring from one church to another are concentrating on fewer churches. Simply stated, a few churches are getting bigger at the expense of smaller churches. While that phenomenon has been in play for quite a while, it is now accelerating. The old barrier that held people in specific churches – family connections, denominational loyalty, and loyalty to a specific congregation – are no longer barriers today. People move with great freedom from church to church.

There has been a reluctance to change.  Churches historically have been slow to change. For most of our American history, the pace of cultural and technological change was sufficiently paced for churches to lag behind only five to ten years. Now churches are lagging twenty to thirty years as the pace of change increases dramatically. To many attendees and members, the church thus seems increasingly irrelevant. To be clear, I am speaking about issues of style, methodology, and awareness, not issues of doctrine and biblical truths. A church guest I recently interviewed said it clearly: "I stuck with my parents' church as long as I could.  When we had a big blow up over projection screens in the worship center, I had enough!  I wanted to go to a church where minutia were not issues to fight over." [6]

**Legacy Churches**

In retirement I have worked part-time for a hospital chaplaincy service.  The ministry I work for primarily services long-term acute care hospitals (LTAC's).  I quite regularly find myself ministering to families around the bedside of a dying or recently deceased relative.  I usually try to get them to talk about the loved one, helping them

---

[6] https://thomrainer.com/2016matters o/09/five-reason-church-dying-today

to focus on the good memories of that individual.  I help them focus on what that individual and what they brought to their lives and the lives of others.  At an appropriate point I remind them of their responsibility to live the legacy of the deceased.

As a person of faith, I sincerely want to leave a legacy of faith with those who know and love me.  The older I get, the more I think about such things.  We are all terminal individuals.  Our lives are but a flicker in God's eye.  In word of the psalmist, "As for man, his days are like grass, he flourishes like a flower of the field, the wind blows over it, and it is gone." (Psalm 103:15-16)  My desire is that after my life has ended, those who lives I have touched will somehow carry on my legacy.  I am a child of God.  I have lived under God's grace, and tried to share the hope that brings with those I have met.  I pray that legacy lives on long after I am gone.

A local church, as a community of faith, is also like a living organism.  People of faith gather together to worship and celebrate the sacraments.  They celebrate the blessings and mourn each loss together.  The reality is that every church, this side of heaven is temporary.  Some churches survive for centuries, others exist for only a few years.  The important thing is for the individuals who are part of that community to be aware of and accept the reality that the church they know and love is dying.  Like in the death of a human, the best approach it is to acknowledge what is happening, and focus on the hope we have in Jesus.  Once we have accepted that, we can begin to consider the legacy we want to leave behind.

Steve Gray and Franklin Dumond have dedicated a whole book to the concept of a "legacy church."  In their words, "So, to leave a legacy is to pass on to future generations something of great significance.  Leaving a legacy should be the hope of every church.  The simplest way for an aging church in the final stages of life to leave that legacy is through giving birth to another church."

While many churches exist for years, and maybe even decades, in denial,   Somewhere in that process, legacy churches acknowledge the reality and make plans to die with dignity, and in the process leave a legacy.

First Lutheran Church in Towson, Maryland is an example of a legacy church.  Like many churches in Baltimore County they had seen years of declining membership and worship.  The congregation had a beautiful sanctuary but week and after week fewer people were present.  At the same, there was one Lutheran ministry in Baltimore County that was growing and flourishing; Concordia Preparatory School.  The school was undergoing an identity crisis of its own.  While it was a Lutheran school, its student body was becoming less Lutheran and much more diverse.  An additional reality was that the many Concordia Prep families had no connection with a worship community.

In the words of Ron Scherch, a member of first Lutheran and part of the committee to develop a plan, they finally identified four options.

1)      Disband

2)      Merge with an existing church

3)      Sell their building but continue to rent the space for worship

4)      Move and plant a new worship community on the Concordia campus.


Ron readily admits the fourth option was the scariest but after a series of meetings it came down to two options, merge or move.  The vote was unanimous to move and use the resources from the sale of the building to start something new.  The next step was to find a pastor who was up to the challenge of starting a new, and very unique ministry.  God answered their call and Rev. Peter Couser accept the challenge to be the new mission developer.


While First Lutheran Church will pass out of existence its legacy will live on in a very unique, and dynamic ministry. Pastor Couser will serve both as a chaplain/pastor to the students and their families, but pastor to a new, yet to be named, worship community.


Good Shepherd Lutheran Church in Azle, Texas is another example of a legacy church.  Good Shepherd had an attractive facility but was facing declining worship attendance.  2018 they were faced with a pastoral vacancy. The reached out to Pastor Steve Sandfort to be their vacancy pastor.

Pastor Steve had been called by Crown of Life Lutheran Church as a mission developer.  Crown of Life was forward seeking enough to give Pastor Steve a blank slate. A second career pastor, and an admitted out of the box thinker, he began a coffee shop ministry in Lake Worth, Texas.  The ministry was called The Edge.  Pastor Steve's goal was to plant a church out of that coffee shop.  Crown of Life continued to partner with him and the worship community grew to the point where it needed more space on Sunday mornings.


Pastor Steve told the leadership at Good Shepherd the only way he could make it work was if he brought his diverse flock with him.  It was the merger of two very different worship communities, one very traditional and the other very unconventional.  Under Pastor Steve's leadership it has worked.  Good Shepherd has called Pastor Steve and rebranded their ministry as The Edge Church.  The management of the coffee shop has transferred to The Edge Church.  The coffee shop ministry continues grow and flourish.  They now operate a food truck and are planning a second location on the campus of The University of Texas at Arlington.

The Edge Church stands as another example of how a church that was once terminal, now exists in a new form. Good Shepherd was a legacy church. The transition has not been easy.  It has taken a major adjustment for a congregation that was used to a very traditional style of worship to get used to Pastor Steve's informal style.  The reality is the message of the Gospel is still there and the theology is still the same.  It is just packaged in a way that fits the changing times and the needs of contemporary people.

Legacy churches are an important part of the future of Christianity in America.  As a result of the Pandemic of 2020, it is projected that up to one third of the churches in the United States will close in the next two years.  While that is hard to accept, would it not be a blessing if every one of those terminal churches acknowledged the reality of their circumstances and in the midst of mourning, began to plan to leave a legacy.

From my perspective, the easy route is to just close and merge with another congregation.  The more challenging task is to start something new and different.  The only way that God's Kingdom is really going to expand and reach the lost, is if more terminal churches seek new and unique ways to be Jesus in their community.

# CHAPTER 4

# Mainline Denominations are Going Away

"Christians recently celebrated Easter, a Sunday where many churches

are robust and full. But if current trends continue,

mainline Protestantism has about 23 Easters left."[7]

The above quote appeared in an article in the April 28, 2017 edition of the Washington Post. As a member of a mainline Protestant denomination, in my case the Lutheran Church Missouri Synod, the statement is disturbing! I love my church. I have been on the ministry roster of the LCMS for over fifty years. In retirement, I depend on the church retirement plan to support me now and in the future. The possible end of my church body is not something I want to think about.

It would be easy to dismiss the above statement if it came from a sociologist who was only looking at things from a purely secular perspective. "They don't understand the power of the Gospel," we think. "When you consider the history of the church, they can't be serious," we say. People outside the church are always casting aspersions our way. You might be surprised that the source of the above quote was Ed Stetzer, a pastor, church planter and leader in the missional church movement. Ed Stetzer occupies the Billy Graham Distinguished Chair of Church Mission and Evangelism at Wheaton College. As Executive Director of the Billy Graham Center at the college, he has to be considered a respected voice.

---

In some ways, Ed Stetzer was using shock value to gain our attention. "Ultimately, mainline Protestants likely do have many more than 23 Easters left," Ed Stetzer goes on to say. "Churches will be restarted and revitalized and there will be advancement initiatives. Mainline Protestants won't cease to exist completely in 23 years because the trend will probably slow, but the data does not give us good hope for their future," he concludes.

While you might breathe a sigh of relief knowing Ed Stetzer's quote is intended more as a wake-up call than a verdict, the reality is some mainline denominations will eventually go away. The statistics are not in their favor. Across the board, every mainline Protestant denomination has been in decline for decades. There is no sign of the trend reversing. Non-denominational Mega Churches are growing. Most neighboring traditional, denominational churches have plateaued or are declining.

Reggie McNeal, another voice for the missional movement, echoes Ed Stetzer's thoughts. "With the collapse of the church culture eminent, it makes little sense to continue to pour all ministry efforts on the institutional church."[8] A reality is the mainline denominational churches that are growing have been functioning independently for decades. They long ago stopped using the resources and curriculum produced by a denominational office. Many of them have taken on the style and feel of a Mega Church, while retaining their theological roots. Those churches do not need, and in fact often feel hindered by, a denominational structure and the politics that comes with it.

---

[8] Reggie McNeal, The Present Future, Page 26

# Denominational Decline: Blame it on the Boomers

Jonathan was born in 1950.  He not only grew up in a Christian home, both his parents were in full-time ministry.  His dad was a senior pastor at a large Lutheran Church in Houston.  His mom was a counselor who worked for a Christian based ministry.  Jonathan had gone to a Lutheran grade school and graduated from a Lutheran High School.  He wanted to study business, and as an honor student, had his choice of colleges.  He chose a state university with a great reputation.  Having grown up going to church, he tried the campus Lutheran chapel. He had been introduced to guitar-led worship by the youth director at his church.  He preferred a more casual style of worship, but the chapel only offered a traditional service.  He stopped going because he felt no connection with the rest of the students who seemed more comfortable with liturgical worship.

Jonathan had a fair number of Christian friends and even some from his high school.  That group was attending a large non-denominational church that had a dynamic college ministry that met every Wednesday night.  It was there that he met Allie.  She had grown up in the Baptist Church but was drawn to the college ministry.  Jonathan and Allie quickly fell into a serious relationship. During their senior year, they got engaged and began planning a wedding.  Jonathan's family adored Allie and the feeling was mutual.  Having the ceremony at the church where Jonathan's dad served as pastor just made sense.

After the wedding, Jonathan and Allie moved to Dallas where he had accepted a great job.  There were also a lot of options when it came to studying for his MBA.  Allie found a teaching position at a suburban school district.  They settled into their first apartment with a list of things they needed to do.  Near the top was finding a worship community like the one they had experienced in college.

Several of Jonathan's friends attended a large Bible Church, which was close to their apartment.  Allie soon discovered one of her colleagues worshipped there as well.  They soon became active members and even became small group leaders, hosting a Bible study in their apartment complex.


* * * *


While the previous story is fictional, the scenario is one that has been lived out over and over.  It takes the fingers on both my hands to count the number of friends in the ministry whose offspring have married and chosen to attend a non-denominational "mega church," rather than the traditional denominational church.

In his book, The Next Generation, Paul Taylor references New York Times' columnist, David Brooks.  David Brooks was curious about the religious background of the U. S. presidents.  George W. Bush is one example.  George W. Bush was born into an Episcopal Family but grew up attending a Presbyterian Church.  Now he is a Methodist.  Paul Taylor notes, "In most of the world such faith-hopping would be unheard of.  In America it is practically routine." [9]

The pattern of faith-hopping can really be traced back to the Baby Boomers.  According to David Kinnaman, President of the Barna Group, "essentially Boomers popularized the church dropout phenomenon."[10]   In many ways, Millennials and Gen Z's are mirroring the behavior of their parents. They are either dropping out of

---

[9] The Next Generation, Paul Taylor, 2014
[10] You Lost Me, David Kinnaman, Page 45

the mainline denominations or redefining their faith in a non-denominational context.   That makes sense to me. Mainline denominations peaked in the late sixties/early seventies and have been in a downward trend ever sense. That parallels the time when Baby Boomers were getting married and starting families.  When a couple from two different denominational traditions married, rather than join one of those they look for a middle ground.

## Denominations are Getting Grayer

While I am a Baby Boomer and card-carrying member of AARP, I seriously do not enjoy hanging out with older adults.  My struggle comes from the certainty that the conversation will center around one of three topics: health issues, politics and "the good old days."  That is not my style.  Yes, I am getting older and with that comes physical challenges, but I am okay with that.  It is what it is; so why talk about it.  Secondly, I have a policy, I do not discuss politics.  With regards to "the good old days" yes, I have a lot of memories but those are in the past. My focus is on the future and trying to pass my faith heritage to the next generation, especially my four grandsons.

This creates a problem for me when I visit a church.  The folks are welcoming but quite frankly most of them are my age and the conversation centers on the three topics I try to avoid. I am left to wonder; if I get that feeling, how would a young adult feel entering into that situation? The reality is they have probably checked out the church website and made the decision to avoid it.

Millennials and Gen Z's make up the two largest generational groups.  Companies invest millions of dollars in order to market products and services to those under the age of forty.  In the midst of this realty, many traditional mainline Protestant denominations that are rooted in the past, and are not prepared for what lies ahead.  Much of this is entrenched in the reality that we are a "graying" church.

"The Pew Research data also shows a wide gap between older Americans (Baby Boomers and members of the Silent Generation) and Millennials in their levels of religious affiliation and attendance.  While eight-in-ten members of the Silent Generation (those born between 1928 and 1945) describe themselves as Christians (84%), as do three-quarters of Baby Boomers (76%), only half of Millennials (49%) describe themselves as Christians.  Four-in-ten Millennials identify as unaffiliated." [11]

A 2014 comprehensive study by Pew Research brought to light the generational gap when it came to most mainline Protestant denominations.  The study defined five generational groups:

| | |
|---|---|
| Greatest Generation | Before 1925 |
| Silent Generation | Pre WW II, 1925-1945 |
| Baby Boomers | Post WW II,1946-1968 |
| Generation X | 1969-1980 |
| Millennials | 1980-1995 |

In 2014, Seventy percent (70%) of Episcopalians were over the age of fifty.  Members of Generation X (18%)

---

[11] http://www.pewforum.org/2019/10/17/acknowledgements-38.

and Millennials (12%) made up the remainder of the denomination.

The Presbyterian Church U.S.A. had very similar numbers. Sixty-eight percent (68%) of Presbyterians were over the age of fifty, with a similar 12% of Millennials and 21% of members of Generation X making up the remainder.

My own denomination, the Lutheran Church Missouri Synod, fared slightly better. Fifty-nine percent (59%) of the membership was over the age of fifty, with Baby Boomers making up the largest portion (36%). Members of Generation X made up 28% and Millennials comprised the other 13%.

The fact remains, across the board denominational churches are primarily made up of older, or soon to be "older" adults.

## Denominations are Part of the Past, Not the Future

Presbyterians trace their roots to a Frenchman, John Calvin. John and Charles Wesley, considered the founders of the Methodist movement, attended Oxford University in England. Martin Luther, the Father of the Reformation, and the patriarch of the denomination that bears his name, was a German. All of that means very little to the young believers who are looking for a place where they can grow in their discipleship and network with friends. The bottom line is tradition and their parent's faith can mean little to them. If we cannot retain the young people who grew up in the church, how can we expect to reach the unchurched young people.

Unfortunately, in the past the focus has been more on protecting denominational traditions than it has been carrying the Gospel message into the future.  As we have focused on preserving practices and rituals, we have lost sight of the "main thing."  The church is called to be Jesus in a changing world.  The culture might shift, but the need for the hope found only in Jesus remains the same.  The way that message is packaged and delivered must be constantly changing.

In conclusion I would like to mirror the words of the disciple Peter when he confessed, "You are the Messiah, the Son of the Living God" (Matthew 16:16).  In response, Jesus makes it clear that the church is built on that fact and "the gates of Hades" will not overcome it (Matthew 16:18).  So, I wait in anticipation to see what is next for the church.

# Chapter 5

# The End of the Parish Ministry Model

Resurrection Lutheran Church was founded by a group of German immigrants in 1910. The church was located in a neighborhood close to the downtown district of a major U.S. city. All of the founding families were middle class, with the men working in some of the factories located nearby. The women were stay-at-home moms. The small congregation initially worshiped in homes but soon had enough money to purchase a small house that they converted into their first church.

Rev. Edmund Schulte was the first pastor. A compassionate, soft-spoken man, Pastor Schulte guided the small flock through the 20's and the Great Depression. In the mid 1930's, the church made the decision to purchase the facilities of a neighboring Methodist Church that had outgrown the space. The three hundred seat sanctuary was more than adequate and the basement served as a fellowship hall. An attached education wing contained Sunday school classrooms and a youth room. At this point, Sunday worship attendance averaged around 250, with almost 150 children in Sunday school.

Pastor Schulte's oldest son, August, felt called to go into the pastoral ministry. When he graduated from the seminary in 1937, the congregation called him to be their assistant pastor, with the plan for him to succeed his father. Unlike his dad, Gus Schulte was a dynamic personality.  His outgoing nature made him popular with the younger members of the church.  Part of his initial job description was working with the church youth and young adult groups.  Both flourished under his leadership and soon many young people from the neighborhood were attending his Wednesday night youth fellowship event, that featured a meal and Bible study.  The Sunday school also experienced growth under "Pastor Gus'" leadership.  He led the spirited opening worship for the children's Sunday school each week.  One highlight for the kids each week was the celebration of birthdays and the recognition of attendance awards.  It was rare for a child to miss a Sunday.  Achieving a year's perfect attendance meant your name was entered into a drawing for a new Schwinn Bike, a contribution from a member who owned a Bike Shop.

After World War II, the congregation continued to experience growth.  The children who were attracted to Sunday school and youth group brought their parents with them.  The two Sunday morning services were full, the classroom building barely held the expanding education ministry.  The congregational leadership decided to respond to the challenge by constructing a new education wing and a community center that would feature a full-size gym.

Resurrection Lutheran Church really flourished in the 50's and the 60's.  The new facility allowed them to expand both their ministry to children and to youth. They operated a neighborhood basketball league and their church softball teams won city championships. Their annual Vacation Bible School attracted over 500 children.  Many of the children were funneled into the

confirmation program, which led to church membership.
It was not uncommon for there to be fifty or more
children in the 8th grade confirmation class.  The church
added a Saturday evening service and an additional
Sunday morning service to accommodate the crowds.


Resurrection had more than a dynamic education and
youth ministry.  The music ministry grew to include
multiple choirs.  The men's club met monthly.  They
hosted an annual sports banquet featuring professional
athletes and a golf tournament.  They also had multiple
bowling teams.  The ladies aid held an annual Christmas
Craft Fair that attracted throngs. They also held rummage
sales and bake sales during the year.  At one point, the
full-time staff numbered over a dozen.


That was then!  Today, less than thirty people drive in
every Sunday to worship in the sanctuary.  They have not
had a full-time pastor in ten years, depending on a series
of retired clergy to fill the pulpit on Sunday.  The once
active education and community center is vacant.  A
charter school had rented the building for a number of
years but closed due to declining enrollment.  The city
had rented the space for a homeless shelter for a couple
of winters. The deteriorating building eventually did not
meet their operating standards.  Since no one had the
funds to bring the building up to code the program
closed. The few remaining members know their days are
numbered.  Attempts to sell the facilities have also failed.
They know the day is coming when they will have to turn
off the lights for the last time and walk away!

* * * *

The above story, while fictional, is lived out with regularity.  As I drive around north Dallas, I cannot go a mile without seeing at least one "Church of the Shattered Dreams."  Some congregations have closed, and others are barely hanging on.  The facilities all look familiar. There is a sanctuary, fellowship hall and education wing. They are surrounded by parking lots that were once full, but now stand empty.  They all represent the past way of doing "parish ministry."  You put up a church in a neighborhood.  You add Sunday school classrooms and a youth center, and people will come.  The "Field of Dreams" approach might work in the movies and for the church fifty years ago but in the real world 2020 edition, building it does not guarantee they will come.


## History Lesson

In many ways, the concept of parish ministry or the parish church can be traced back to Europe.  Prior to the Reformation, the only option was a Catholic Church. Post Reformation, people had an option.  They could continue to worship at the Catholic Cathedral or at the Protestant Church.  It was the persecution of those who chose the Protestant road that led to the church coming to America.  Here, there was religious freedom.  Initially, the communities shared an ethnic heritage, and the local church reflected that.


In most towns, churches of various denominations were built to accommodate those of various ethnicities.  Drive through most small towns today and you still have remnants of those silos.  Often the Catholic, Methodist,

Baptist, Lutheran and other churches were located in close proximity.

As towns grew into cities, the same concept held true. Now the churches were built in neighborhoods. Most mainline denominations tried to build churches within walking distance of their parishioners. Growing up on the eastside of Detroit, there were at least six churches representing different denominations within a ten-minute walk of our house.

That was then, but this is now. In his book Joining Jesus on His Mission, Greg Finke writes, "For a very long time the U.S. church was well-built, well positioned and doing an excellent job of meeting the spiritual needs of a largely churched culture." [12] Greg Finke also notes that over the last forty years a "cultural hurricane" has changed the landscape. As a result, the "river of culture" no longer flows through the parish church.

The church scene has changed since 1980. The establishment of the Mega Church has changed the model of how to do ministry. In my hometown of Dallas, churches like Watermark, Gateway, and Fellowship now carry out the kind of ministry that Resurrection Lutheran Church once had.

In the contemporary world where marketing and image are so important, Millennials and Gen Z's are searching for a sense of community. Mega Churches can better meet their needs in much the same way neighborhood parish churches did in the 50's and the 60's. You can find

---

[12] Joining Jesus on His Mission, Greg Finke, 2014, Page 39

a health club, coffee shop, Bible study, support group
and child-care all in the same place where you worship.
Churches holding on to the now outdated parish model
will find themselves on the sidelines.

## Sunday School

The traditional Sunday school stands as a good example
of how the culture has shifted.  The Sunday school was a
big part of the ministry of fictional Resurrection Lutheran
Church, as it was in almost every church in the 50's, the
60's and even the 70"'s.

I served a church that had a dynamic Sunday school.
From 1972-1980, I was director of Christian education
(DCE) at Immanuel Lutheran Church in Downers
Grove, Illinois.  Rally Day marked the beginning of a new
Sunday school year.  During the month of August, I sent
"Calls to Teach" to each of the candidates for the various
teaching positions.  Recruitment was easy.  There was
very little turnover from year to year.  Teachers were
required to attend a meeting at the beginning of each
month where the pastor and I would prepare them for
the next four lessons in the rotation.  There were two
teachers for each grade, with most classes averaging
twelve to fifteen students.

In 1980, I found a similar situation when I moved to
Bethlehem Lutheran Church in Dundee, Illinois but the
winds of change were coming.  By the mid 80's, it had
become more difficult to recruit teachers and attendance
among the children was becoming more sporadic.  When

we moved to Dallas in 1988, I found a similar situation at Holy Cross Lutheran Church.

I was not the only one observing such a decline.  In a 2015 article, USA Today noted that, between 1997 and 2004, churches lost tens of thousands of Sunday school programs.  Using data from the Barna Group, they reported how enrollment had fallen across denominations. From 2004 to 2010, for example, Sunday school attendance dropped nearly 40 percent among Evangelical Lutheran churches in America and almost 8 percent among Southern Baptist churches.[13]

* * * *

I have focused on the ministry of the Sunday school since it not only is a ministry that is in decline but also because it has lost its sense of purpose.  To understand this sense of purpose, we need to explore the history of the Sunday school.  Sunday school as a ministry traces its roots to Gloucester, England in the mid eighteenth century. Robert Raikes owned a printing business he had inherited from his father.  Robert, a Christian, was moved by the plight of the Children of Gloucester who were victims of the lack of child labor laws.  He saw schooling as the best intervention. He shared the idea with his pastor and friend, Reverend Thomas Stock.  Together they decided the best available time was Sunday as the children were often working in the factories the other six days. The best available teachers were lay people. The textbook was the Bible! The intended curriculum started with learning to read and then progressed to the catechism. [14]

[13] www.usatoday.com/story/news/nation/2015/03/22
[14] John Carroll Power, The Rise and Progress of the Sunday School, A Biography of

Over time, we have turned what was intended as a
ministry to the lost children of the community into a
program to educate the offspring of parents who are
already members.  The focus has shifted from outreach
to just serving member families.  True, the church is to
teach and equip people to share the love of Jesus, but we
are also called to be Jesus in the world.  Within the parish
ministry model, the emphasis has shifted from being
Jesus in the community to meeting the needs of those
who are already inside the walls of the church.

In the end, Sunday school has served us well but it is time
to put it and other components of the parish ministry
model to rest.  The parish church was like a silo.  It
functioned well as a storage container for Christians. Like
a grain silo contains only one kind of grain, the parish silo
holds similar kinds of souls.  The members of the parish
church usually share the same traditions and heritage.  All
the families are typically of the same skin color and
economic status.

We can carry this a step further.  Within the main silo,
that is the parish church, there are other mini silos.
There are separate silos for children's ministry and youth
ministry.  There can be a women's guild and a men's
club.  We can go further and add other silos like the
music ministry and the usher's club.  All too often these
ministries compete against each other for budget money
and to capture the interest of volunteers.  The end result
has often been a contentious relationship between

competing activities, instead of working together to build the kingdom.  People were busy filling their silos.


It is long past the time when we should have dismantled those silos.  There is no future in traditional parish ministry.

# CHAPTER 6

## Fewer Pastors: More Ministers

Holcum, Texas is located on Highway 287, about thirty-five miles west of Wichita Falls and one hundred and sixty miles northwest of Dallas-Fort Worth. The population peaked at 3,500 in the late 60's. The town is named after Lyle Holcum who was a rancher who settled there. Located on the Santa Fe Railroad mainline, the town once had its own train station and livestock yard. Holcum serviced the needs of the farmers and ranchers who lived in that area of north-central Texas. The stockyard closed in 1968 when the railroad eliminated the stop and that began the decline. Folks started to drive to Wichita Falls not only to sell their livestock and crops but also to do their shopping. Eventually, most of the stores closed and the town bank merged with a larger bank in Wichita Falls. Today, Main Street is just a row of empty stores. Many of the 2,100 folks who live there now commute to Wichita Falls to work.

The history of Trinity Church parallels the town. Membership peaked at 300 in the early 70's but steadily declined from there. For decades, Pastor August Moerbe was the pastor. When he retired in 1981, the church chose to call a young pastor from the seminary to replace him. That pastor stayed a couple of years after which the church went through another vacancy before another young pastor arrived. This became the pattern, as they had trouble maintaining continuity in the leadership. As the community declined, so did the church.

When Sunday attendance dropped below twenty people in 2010, the church voted to close. They could no longer afford to pay a pastor and the church building was deteriorating around them.  They decided to merge with the nearby church in the town of Electra.  Four of the remaining families joined that church but the other three families decided to keep worshiping in the home of one of the members.  Two of the families had young children and the other family was an older couple, the parents of one of the husbands.  One of the dads had served as an elder in the former congregation.  The other had regularly led the Sunday adult Bible class.

The three families felt they could not only continue to worship but also invite other families to join them.  So began a new worship community.  They invited unchurched neighbors and soon outgrew the home where they were meeting.  They arranged to move their Sunday morning services to the town hall, using the adjoining park with its pavilion for a fellowship potluck following the services.  The former elder continues to serve as the worship leader, and several of the moms have organized classes for the children and the teens.  The church continued to follow the doctrine of the denomination they left.

Today, almost a hundred people gather on Sunday morning for worship and fellowship.  They also gained permission from the town to use the town hall for an after school tutoring program.  The older couple that were a part of the original core group recruited other older adults to come along-side them to staff the program.  Daily, over fifty children from the school located a block away come to be a part of the program.

While no longer affiliated with a church body, Holcum Community Church is very much alive.  There are plans to remodel one of the vacant downtown stores to make it a worship center and a more permanent location for the after-school program.  There are also plans to partner

with the food bank in Wichita Falls to establish a branch
in Holcum that would be operated by volunteers from
the church.

While the previous story is fictional, the concept is very
realistic.  It is a response to two very real problems: 1)
Many small town and even urban churches are dying.  2)
There are fewer pastors to serve the remaining churches;
much less the small worship communities that still exist.


* * * *


In 1973, Oscar Feucht broke new ground when it came
to discipleship in his book, Everyone a Minister.  In
preparation for this chapter, I reread Oscar Feucht's
book.  The opening paragraph sounds so familiar, yet it
was written in the early seventies.


"The church of the 1970's is experiencing a crisis which
is unprecedented in modern times.  In some instances,
the exodus from church is considerably larger than the
growth of new members.  One large American Protestant
denomination recently reported a loss of 40,000
members in a single year.  The graph on membership
growth and church attendance of many Protestant groups
of the last few years shows a straight line indicating a
holding operation or they show a downward curve." [15]


Oscar Feucht's proposed solution to the crisis was found
in the doctrine of the "Priesthood of all Believers."  He
explores how it is a New Testament concept.  He begins

---

[15] Oscar Feucht, Everyone a Minister, 1974, Page 11

by exploring 1 Peter 2:4-10.  Peter states we must "Come to the living Stone rejected as worthless by man, but chosen as valuable to God." (vs. 4 TEV)   In the process, Peter continues, we will become "Living Stones" for the building of a "spiritual house." [16]

Oscar Feucht further states that while we will never find the word "church member" in the Bible, we will consistently find the word "disciple" used throughout the New Testament.  He further outlines a "ministry of the laity" which in the end is not that much different than that of the clergy.  We are called to be Jesus in the world.  [17]

What Oscar Feucht was calling for is what we are experiencing today in the missional movement.  The church equips and sends people to be missionaries in their neighborhoods, workplaces and at the local Starbucks.  Every interaction is an opportunity to ask people to come along side us in a Gospel-changing relationship with Jesus Christ.

*  *  *  *

At the time Oscar Feucht's book came out, I was serving as a Director of Christian Education (DCE) at a church in the Chicago suburb of Downers Grove.  At the beginning of a monthly meeting, I recall the spirited discussion the pastor and I had with our elders as they processed that book.  I applied some of Oscar Feucht's principles in my ministry.  Our Sunday school and vacation Bible school teachers all received an annual "Call to Teach."  I was able to order an official looking "call" document that

---

[16] Everyone a Minister, Page 36
[17] Everyone a Minister, Page 78

each of them received annually.  The form was available from Concordia Publishing House (CPH) along with our teaching resources.  The document was indeed similar to the one a pastor and other professional Lutheran ministers received when called to a position.  I viewed each of my volunteers as a "called teacher" and their work was an extension of my ministry as part of the Body of Christ.

Somewhere in the late 70's those "Call to Teach" forms disappeared.  There were some that took offense that a Lutheran publishing company would offer a resource that would promote the idea that volunteer teachers and pastors were indeed called in the same way

It seemed that some disagreed with Oscar Feucht's belief that "Everyone is a Minister."  There were indeed classifications, or a hierarchy, when it came to discipleship.  Individual church members could be teachers, plumbers, nurses and lawyers, but they could never be "real" ministers.


## The Missional Movement

Thankfully, things have changed.  There is a new, fresh, wind that is blowing through the Christian Church.  The missional church movement arose in 1998 when a group of six Protestant theologians published a book entitled *Missional Church: A Vision for the Sending of the Church in North America.*[18]  Church membership continued to decline despite the "church growth movement" of the 80's.  While Church Growth strategies were intended to bring people into the church, the Missional Movement proposed that all members go out into the world and reflect the gospel in their surrounding

---

[18] http://www.thearda,com/timeline/movement_24.asp

communities.  Instead of inviting people in, the new movement encouraged people to be Jesus and build community where they lived.

The church has always referred to Matthew 28:19-20 as Jesus' "Great Commission."  For centuries, we have, unfortunately, seen this command as a call to "the church" to baptize, teach and make disciples.  The Missional Movement moved the responsibility away from "the church" to individual members of the body.  We are all called to be missionaries to those around us.

Reggie McNeal was one of the early leaders in the Missional Church Movement.  His 2003 book The Present Future begins with a reality check; "The current church culture in North America is on life support.  It is living off the work, money, and energy of previous generations from a previous world order.[19]  Reggie McNeal spends much of his book focusing on "the emergence of a new world."  "The church of Jesus is moving into the postmodern world," he notes.[20]  Indeed, missional Jesus means being Jesus to those around me, and in the process, inviting them to come along side me as a disciple.

Greg Finke expanded on this concept in his 2013 book Joining Jesus on His Mission; How to Be an Everyday Missionary.  Greg Finke poses the question: "Did Jesus choose to hang out with people in spite of having a huge mission with limited time or because he had a huge mission with limited time.  In my view, he hung out with people because of it.[21]  Being a missionary for Jesus simply means being Jesus where you are, and inviting other people to come along side you on your walk.

---

19 Reggie McNeal, Present Future, 2003, Page 1
20 Present Future, Page 2
21 Greg Finke, Joining Jesus on His Mission, 2013, Page 58

I am often invited to speak to groups. When I share this concept the question "how do I do this" ultimately arises. My response is always the same; how different would your life be if you moved your grill and lawn chairs to your front yard? One reality of our North Dallas culture is most people live in homes where the backyards have privacy fences. As a result, we do not know our neighbors.

I grew up on the eastside of Detroit. We knew our neighbors because our front porches were gathering spots. Hanging out in your front yard is one step toward living missionally. People still walk their dogs and have to cut their lawns and trim their hedges. If we get to know our neighbors, maybe they will get to know the Jesus in us. That could lead to sharing concerns, praying together and maybe even a neighborhood Bible study.

The fictional story at the beginning of this chapter is a good example of people living missionally. Three families decided to venture out on their own and get to know their community. In the process, a new worship community developed and a whole town was impacted.

The equipping of people to be disciples and missionaries to their communities is critical at a time when there are fewer and fewer ordained ministers.

**Fewer Pastors**

My own denomination, The Lutheran Church Missouri Synod (LCMS), has a critical shortage of pastors. In 2019, our denomination had 5,991 congregations. We had 6,077 ordained pastors. On paper that seems like an equal number, but it does not tell the whole picture.

Three hundred and twenty-two (322) of the ordained pastors listed were specific ministry pastors (SMP), meaning they served under the supervision of an administrative pastor. In addition, some ordained pastors are teaching at colleges and seminaries. Still other pastors serve in administrative roles. Then you have to add in the fact that many larger churches are served by multiple pastors, you begin to see the problem.

Concordia Theological Seminary in St. Louis is the second oldest seminary in the country. Dating back to 1839, it has long trained pastors for the Lutheran Church Missouri Synod (LCMS), but like many seminaries it has faced declining enrollment. In the Summer 2017 issue of the Concordia Journal, President Dale Meyer addressed the problem. "For some years now, the Council of Presidents has not been able to fill calls for new pastors from the seminaries because there have not been enough graduates from the Master of Divinity programs to meet the needs. The consequences of this shortage are serious to the life of the Synod in many ways, especially because the shortage of pastors jeopardizes faithful pastoral care to people and thereby diminishes vitality and growth in congregations without a pastor." [22]

The situation for the LCMS has not changed much since Rev. Meyer's comments. The November 2019 issue of the Lutheran Witness, an official periodical of the LCMS, focused on the "state of the Synod." Concerning pastoral education, it noted that Concordia Seminary in St. Louis had 566 students, and its sister institution, Concordia Seminary in Fort Wayne had 289 students. While it might sound encouraging, only 355 of those students were pursuing Master of Divinity degrees, leading to becoming parish pastors. Almost half, 304,

---

[22] http://concordiatheology.com/2017/06/low-seminary-enrollments/

were graduate students.   Considering it is a four-year program, that calculates to an average of less than 90 new pastors receiving calls to serve local churches each year. When you add in the reality that many pastors currently serving are over the age of sixty, you begin to get a scope of the problem.  [23]

It is not a problem limited to one church body.  The Barna group has long been tracking the status of pastoral ministry in our country.  When George Barna published his first study in1992, the median age of Protestant clergy was 44 years old. One in three pastors was under the age of 40, and one in four was over 55. Just 6 percent were 65 or older. Twenty-five years later, the average age is 54. Only one in seven pastors is under 40, and half are over 55. The percentage of church leaders 65 and older has nearly tripled, meaning there are more pastors in the oldest age bracket than there are leaders younger than 40. [24]

The Minnesota Star Tribune focused on the problem in August of 2018.  They noted that fewer men and women are willing to take up the calling. The Evangelical Lutheran Church in America (ELCA), for example, reports that 3,661 pastors have retired since 2010, but only 2,241 new minsters have been ordained. Additionally, three out of four of Minnesota's 962 Catholic priests are now classified as retired or disabled, and not working full time. Nationally, 60 percent of Catholic priests fall into the "retired" or "disabled" category.  [25]

* * * *

---

[23] Lutheran Witness, November, 2019, Page 7
[24] http://Barna.com/stateofthechurch/
[25] http://startribune.com/fewer-men-and-women-are-entering-the-seminary/490381681/

There can be little doubt that the church of the future will look vastly different.  While mega churches and cornerstone churches will continue to be staffed by full-time pastors, there are going to be more small worship communities that function quite well without trained clergy.  Some of those smaller worship communities will exist under the auspices of a local church, but others are going to be independent.

Whether it be through independent churches like the fictional one at the beginning of this chapter, or through house churches or groups that gather at the local Starbucks, the Gospel will be alive and well.

# CHAPTER 7

## The End of Tax-Exempt Status

During his brief run for the presidency in the fall of 2019, former Texas congressman, Beto O'Rourke raised a few eyebrows. He proposed that "religious institutions like colleges, churches and charities should lose their tax-exempt status if they opposed same sex marriage." While Beto O'Rourke's candidacy was short-lived, his pitch to end tax exempt status is not going away.  As the culture shifts more to the left, support for churches and other religious institutions is going to dwindle.  In preparing for the future, churches and church professionals need to consider what life will be like without those benefits.

Beto O'Rourke is not the first politician to call for limiting the special privilege that churches and religious organizations enjoy.  In his State of the Union address in 1875, President Ulysses S. Grant called for "correcting the evil that if permitted to continue could lead to great trouble in our land."  Grant argued that churches received all the "protections and benefits of the government without bearing their proportion of the burdens and expenses for the same." [26]

In many ways, the existence of a tax exemption for churches can be traced back to our nation's European roots.  In Europe, churches that were affiliated with what were referred to as "established" denominations were exempt from paying taxes.  An additional reality is our founding fathers wanted to avoid such "established"

---

churches being supported by taxes leveled on the general public. That could lead to what they perceived as governmental control over the church. Thomas Jefferson and others wanted to avoid that; hence, separation of church and state became one of our founding principles. [27]

The waves of change began in 1983 with the case of Bob Jones University vs. the United States. Bob Jones University had a ban on interracial dating. The school claimed that stance was rooted in religious beliefs and as such was protected by the First Amendment of the U.S. Constitution. The school lost the case when the courts ruled "infringement on religious liberty could be justified when necessary to accomplish an overriding government interest, in this case end racial segregation." [28]

While conservative movements, like the Moral Majority, had existed prior to the Bob Jones University case, the court's decision caused them to ramp-up their efforts. It seemed like almost overnight, during the presidency of Ronald Reagan, the conservative religious voice became an influence in the political arena. Many on the political left began to question whether the line between church and state had been violated.

Both James Dobson's ministry, Family Talk Action, and Franklin Graham's Samaritan Purse came under IRS scrutiny during the Barrack Obama administration: another indication of things to come. [29]

When you consider the current political climate, the distrust that many young voters have toward the church and other established institutions, we cannot continue to be optimistic about the church and the tax exemption

---

[27] Kermit D. Hall, editor, The Oxford Companion to the Supreme Court of the United States, pages 717 ff
[28] Christianity Today, January/February 2020, Page 46
[29] Christianity Today, January/February 2020, Page 47

status it has enjoyed for centuries. This is not 17th Century Europe when churches were part of the culture. This is not even 20th Century America when the church was part of the mainstream. We live in the Post-Christian 21st Century. According to The Center for the Study of Global Christianity at Gordon-Cromwell Seminary, as of 2020, only 9% of the Christians in the world live in North America. The bulk of those claiming Jesus as their Savior live in Africa (26%) and Latin America (25%). Christianity in America in particular is in a steep decline. According to Pew Research, 43% of Americans claimed to be Protestants in 2019, down from 51% in 2009. [30]

In this political and societal context, we are naïve in believing the tax-exempt status the church has always enjoyed will continue in the future.

*  *  *  *

If indeed churches lose their tax-exempt status, there will be some heavy consequences. In his book Rising Tides, Neil Cole identifies three of those implications:

> Loss of clergy housing allowance

> Loss of the property tax exemption on churches

> Removal of the tax deduction for contributions [31]

**Clergy Housing Allowance**

---

[30] www.pewforum.org/2019/10/17/acknowledgments-38/.
[31] Neil Cole, Rising Tides, 2018, Page 62

Let me begin with some words that at least for the immediate future might be encouraging. Neil Cole wrote his book prior to a major court decision. The Freedom From Religion Foundation (FFRF), an atheist organization, had brought the most recent lawsuit challenging clergy housing allowance. In March of 2018, the U.S. Court of Appeals for the Seventh Circuit in Chicago ruled the clergy housing allowance to be constitutionally permissible. Still, churches should be aware that the clergy housing allowance could be headed for more challenges in the future.


In a statement after the March decision by the U.S. Court of Appeals for the Seventh Circuit in Chicago, the FFRF urged Congress to take the opportunity and intervene by repealing Section 107(2), the Tax Code provision that makes the clergy housing allowance possible. In a tweet, the Associated Press said FFRF is "reviewing options." [32]T he Chicago Tribune quoted FFRF Co-president, Annie Laurie Gaylor, who calls it the foundation's "David vs. Goliath fight," because the housing allowance is supported by virtually every organized religion, who stated that, "The government is showing a preference for religion over non-religion," she continued. "The rest of us pay more because ministers pay less. If these ministers were so concerned about social welfare, they should be paying their taxes. They're robbing the treasury of certain taxes that should go to help everybody." [33]

---

[32] (https://www.churchlawandtax.com/blog/2019/march/seventh-circuit-clergy-housing-allowance-is-constitutional.html)
[33] (https://www.chicagotribune.com/news/ct-met-church-tax-housing-allowance-lawsuit-20181023-story.html)

Shortly after the court ruling, church consultant, Thom
Rainer offered these words of warning, "If you're getting a
minster's housing allowance right now, I encourage you
to live like you're not—because it will eventually go away.
The housing allowance is the most amazing tax benefit
ministers receive." [34]

## Property Tax Exemption

Prestonwood Baptist Church is located on 140 acres of
prime real estate in Plano, Texas.  It is located within
walking distance of the upscale Willow Bend Mall where
people can shop at Macys or families can visit the Crayola
Experience.  The church is surrounded by restaurants,
businesses and services that cater to the wealthy.
Prestonwood Baptist is a bit like a mall itself.  You will
find a health club, bookstore and food court all on their
campus.  They also offer day care and operate an
academy that educates children from pre-school through
high school.

North of Prestonwood Baptist sit many upscale
residential neighborhoods.  I doubt if you could find any
home in that vicinity that would be valued under
$500,000.  Land is costly in Plano, Texas.  Most of the
homes are located on small lots, with limited yard space.
The residents of those homes pay dearly in property tax
to live in Plano, Texas.  In return, they receive the best in
city services like police and fire protection, in addition to

---

[34] (https://thomrainer.com/2018/04/will-ministers-housing-allowance-go-away-rainer-leadership-421/)

excellent schools.  In the same way, all the businesses that surround the church pay taxes to the city.

In his book Rising Tides, Neil Cole referenced the ministry of Joel Osteen's Lakewood Church in Houston, Texas.  Lakewood Church worships in an arena that once was home to the Houston Rockets basketball team.  Lakewood Church generates $32 million dollars per year income, but like other churches in this country, pays no property tax. [35]

Do not get me wrong.  Churches bring a lot of benefits to the community in terms of ministry and services, but then so do Starbucks coffee shops.  I spend a lot of time writing and networking with folks in Starbucks.  They offer free workspace; okay it cost me a couple of bucks for coffee.  I see a lot of folks around me holding meetings and even small group Bible studies.  My local Starbucks is busy and keeps a lot of young people gainfully employed.  Starbucks gives a lot back to the community, and they are paying dearly in taxes.  My point is, a lot of young folks, and some liberal minded old folks too, are questioning why businesses and corporations are paying their fair share while churches are not.

The January/February 2020 issue of Christianity Today looked at this issue in depth.  The article noted, "By one conservative estimate, federal and state government subsidies amount to an $82.5 billion transfer each year.  Meanwhile, the percentage of Americans reporting no

---

[35] Neil Cole, Rising Tides, page 75

particular religious affiliation continues to rise.  The religious 'nones' now compose 23.1 percent of the population, recently becoming the largest group in the American religious landscape ahead of both Catholics and evangelicals." [36]

Being realistic, I believe churches need to plan now for losing the exemption sometime in the next twenty years.

## Removing Tax Deductions for Contributions

Of the three items identified by Neil Cole, loss of the deduction for charitable contributions is probably the least likely to go away.  There are a couple of reasons for this.

First off, there are too many non-profit organizations and ministries that depend on charitable contributions.  Secondly, no other organization of ministry has the ability to offer what the church offers.  Paul Matzko, a historian of American religion and politics, was recently quoted as stating, "I've never seen any museum serving soup to the hungry."  He further stated, "… there is no museum in Philadelphia where you can drop your kids off at 1:00 p.m. and pick them up again at 6:00 p.m. For churches that is nothing strange." [37]

---

[36] Christianity Today, January/February 2020, Page 48
[37] Christianity Today, January/February 2020, Page 49

Indeed, churches are in a unique position to offer the gifts of compassion, mercy and benevolence to a hurting world.  Whether it be through a food pantry, low cost child care or counseling services, churches need to continue to search for new ways to "be Jesus" in a broken world.  To combat the voices from the left, the church needs to continue to seek new ways to let the world see the "light of Christ" shining bright through us and our ministries.

# CHAPTER 8

## No Future in Brick and Mortar

"Unless the Lord builds the house, the builders labor in vain.

Unless the Lord watches over the city, the watchmen stand guard in vain"

Psalm 127:1

In his 2012 book, Autopsy of a Deceased Church, Thom Rainer takes a close look at the demise of fourteen churches.  He notes early on that one common thread is that the deceased churches "lived with the past as a hero." [38] In almost every case, a building was part of their history. Not only can the upkeep of a decaying building drain a congregation's resources, all too often, those structures can become the focal point of dissention.  Take the following example as Thom Rainer describes his experience touring a deserted building with a former member.

We stopped. The light pointed to a room, a single room. "This is it," he said softly. I could not tell if his tone was respect or sadness. The sign was still on the room: Lydia Room. "This room was the equivalent of a parlor or bride's room in other churches," he offered without any questions from me. "There was a great pride about this room," he said. "It had the nicest furniture. It got first

---

[38] Thom Rainer, Autopsy of a Deceased Church: 12 Ways to Keep Yours Alive (Kindle Edition) location 163

attention before anything else in the church." He continued his story, and it was sadly typical. The room would become the focus of dissension. Who could use it? Who decided what furniture went in there? Could people outside the church use it? Could a normal church fellowship be held there? "The arguments were pretty ugly," he said. "And I don't think I knew it at the time, but looking back, our focus on this room marked the beginning of our steep decline." He paused. "I know we died for a lot of reasons," he offered, "but the fights over this room are the clearest markers I have that point to the closing of the doors. It seems so silly, so sad now. We were fighting over a stupid room while the church died. [39]

The November 2018 issue of The Atlantic Monthly painted a bleak picture of the future of church buildings in America.  It describes one such building in Brooklyn, New York.

"The 19th-century building was once known as St. Vincent De Paul Church and housed a vibrant congregation for more than a century. But attendance dwindled and coffers ran dry by the early 2000s. Rain leaked through holes left by missing shingles, a tree sprouted in the bell tower, and the Brooklyn diocese decided to sell the building to developers. Today, the Spire Lofts boasts 40 luxury apartments, with one-bedroom units renting for as much as $4,812 per month. It takes serious cash to make God's house your own, apparently. Many of our nation's churches can no longer afford to maintain their structures—6,000 to 10,000 churches die each year in America—and that number will likely grow." [40]

---

[39] Thom Rainer, Autopsy of a Deceased Church (Kindle Edition) location 637-646
[40]

A conversation I had with an acquaintance further underscores how a worship community can lose focus when it comes to their connection with a building.  I had not seen this person in a couple of years.  I knew he was part of a congregation that had a proud past, but now faced rapidly declining numbers.  They also worshipped in a stately gothic building that can easily accommodated several hundred worshippers.  When I inquired about his church, he informed me their long-time pastor had retired and now another retired pastor serves them on a part-time basis.  "The only full-time employee is our custodian.  We do need to keep the lights on," he noted.

I came away from that conversation feeling sad.  While I mourned for those few folks who gathered in an empty sanctuary, I grieved even more for the many similar churches.  Those worship communities are sinking.  They cling to the past while missing the hope that lies in the future.

## Jesus did not Give His Life for a Building

Any discussions about the church have to begin with Peter's confession in Matthew 16:13-20. In response to Jesus' question, "Who do you say that I am?" Peter responds, "You are the Christ, the Son of the living God." Jesus makes it clear that his "Church" will be built on this statement (vs. 18).  His church is built on the confession of Peter that Jesus, the Christ, the son of the

---

living God IS THE FOUNDATION OF HIS CHURCH. Furthermore, the Greek word for church is ekklesia which refers to a "community" of faith.  The "people of God" will always stand firm on the "Rock" that is Jesus Christ.

The Christian Church began as a ragtag group of men who were called by their leader, Jesus, to begin a movement.  During their three years together, the twelve disciples, and the other faithful followers, were very much "the church."  They had no building or formal structure, only a Shepherd who was tending, teaching and equipping them for the ministry ahead.

In the garden prior to going to the cross, Jesus prays for those disciples, but he also prayed for you and me. "I do not ask for only these (the disciples) but also for those who will believe me through their word..." (John 17:20). That includes you and me, some of those who have come to know Jesus through the words of the Gospel and through the actions and message of the Apostles.

Any mention of the "church," the ekklesia, is a reference to the Body of Believers.  In Ephesian 2:19-22, Paul writes of how the church is "built on the foundation of the apostles and prophets, with Jesus Christ himself as the chief cornerstone."  The church is a living, breathing body, called to be Jesus in the world.  At no point was the church to ever be a physical structure.  Still, if you were to ask an unbelieving friend to define the church, they would probably almost always point to a building and say, "That's a church."  Oh, how we have misled the world! If you talk to any individual that was part of a church that lost its build, whether by fire or natural disaster, they will assure you the church as the Body of Christ continued to exist.


## Missional Communities don't need Permanent Structures


Church structures will continue to serve a need for mega churches and the cornerstone churches described in chapter two.  There might even be instances where mega churches and cornerstone churches need to expand their facilities to accommodate growth.  I foresee those two types of churches experiencing growth as smaller churches die and the former members look to affiliate with a worship community that has a similar style.  In many ways this is "deceptive growth".  In reality, those new members are already believers; they are just abandoning a sinking ship for another that offers a safer refuge.


The real growth in the kingdom is going to happen outside the walls of a "traditional" sanctuary.  Missional communities are already happening when people of faith live "missionally" in their neighborhoods.  Alan Hirsh was one of the pioneers in the missional movement. Unlike the traditional model that was clergy led, missional communities are lay driven.


Church consultant, Alan Hirsh, raised some eyebrows when he stated, "the prevailing Pastor-Teacher combination is not generative enough for "Movemental Christianity".  The June, 2020 issue of Christianity Today defines "Movemental Christianity" and notes that while the gospel message is unchanging, the way it is expressed and presented will vary from culture to culture. "It also recognizes that, as the people of God, we are called to appropriately identify with those to whom we have been sent."  Simply put, "Movemental Christianity" encourages individual to be Jesus in the community where they live.  In the process they become "the church" in their neighborhood.  Such "churches" do not require a permanent structure. [41]

What Alan Hirsh proposes is much more organic, in contrast to a centralized institution.  Missional communities are "interconnected organisms."  Leaders are lay people who attend worship at a church but also minister within their own neighborhoods.  Over time, they might even spend more time ministering and worshipping in their neighborhoods, than they do at their "church."

## A Decline in Financial Support

Doug Paul is a full time Innovation Strategist who works with pastors, churches and denominational leaders who are looking for insights into what the future holds.  In his The Future of the Church Series, one of his predictions is "There will be a large percentage of church building foreclosures."  He points to a number of contributing factors. Among them is a predicted global recession and the fact that many buildings are over leveraged; they were built for anticipated growth that never happened.

---

[41] Alan Hirsh, The Forgotten Ways; Reactivating the Missional Church, 2007, page 75

There are two other factors that are more generational. Millennial and Gen Z believers are going to have lower incomes than did preceding generations.  They also are not the tithers that their parents and grandparents were. Young believers often come with the attitude that "the church is there to serve them and their needs."  They are often accused of having a sense of entitlement.  That attitude is reflected in their attitude toward the church. They expect to be ministered to, but give little thought to the reality that it takes money to operate the ministry.

An additional factor is that the Builder and Boomer generations put a higher degree of value on church buildings.  They were willing to underwrite the cost because they treasured the structures they had invested in.  Millennials and Gen Z's do not share that feeling.  [42]

* * * *

One growing trend is a shopping mall church.  There are three churches located in the Grand Cities Mall in Grand Forks, North Dakota, and another growing worship community at the Outlets in Loveland, Colorado.[43] When you consider the vacant spaces in many malls, it makes sense for churches to locate there.  It also increases visibility and opens up the opportunity for all kinds of drop-in ministries.

The long-term reality is there is no future in constructing a facility for worship.  If a worship community reaches the point where they need space to gather, there are plenty of empty church buildings available in all shapes and sizes.  A better option, considering the fluidity of Christianity, would be to rent a space that fits your needs.

---

[42] Doug Paul, The Futurist Series: 10 Church Predictions for the Next 10 Years
[43] Thehearald.com

As we move forward, one reality is there is no future in investing money in buildings.  Remember the church of the future is going to more resemble a tent than it will a permanent structure like a silo.  As a result, the church needs to be investing in people, not in brick and mortar.

The long-term reality is there is no future in constructing a facility for worship.  If a worship community reaches the point where they need space to gather, there are plenty of empty church buildings available in all shapes and sizes.  A better option, considering the fluidity of Christianity, would be to rent a space that fits your needs.

As we move forward, there is one reality for churches that have plateaued or are in decline: There is no future in investing money in buildings.  Remember the church of the future is going to more resemble a tent than it will a permanent structure like a silo.  As a result, the church needs to be investing in people, not in brick and mortar.

# CHAPTER 9

## The Acts 2:42 Model

"And they devoted themselves to the apostles' teaching
and the fellowship, to the breaking of bread and the
prayers."

(Acts 2:42 ESV)

In this closing chapter, I want to give you a glimpse of the
church to come.  I believe the church of the future is
going to be built on the model we find in Acts 2:42. It
also requires us to understand that Millennials and Gen
Z's desire community, not the fellowship model that most
churches are currently structured around. The existing
model of fellowship ministry is very good at promoting
and maintaining fellowship within the body of Christ but
lacking when it comes to expanding that community.
The Sunday morning fellowship time, potluck dinners
and even small group ministry all feed the desire
members have to sharing time with "church friends."
Aside from the occasional encouraged or equipped to
share the message of Jesus Christ with the lost.  We need
to redefine the way we do evangelism.

It all begins with God's word.  That is the whole point of
Matthew 13.  The words come right from Jesus himself.
The chapter begins with the parable of the sower and
continues with other examples that stress the value of
God's word: the mustard seed, the yeast, the hidden
treasure and the pearl.  Those who sat at the feet of Jesus
learned the lesson well and became the teachers.  In his
book, Subversive: Living as Agents of Gospel
Transformation, Ed Stetzer begins by talking about "the

seed" as the place where the Kingdom starts.  Ed Stetzer
states, "So our first job as subversive kingdom agents is to
be people who receive the implanted word."  Ed Stetzer
states that conventional Christian living is not just a matter
of checking off boxes: worship, Bible study, and church
activities.   [44]

The keys to growing the kingdom of God in Acts 2:42
begin with the apostle's teaching, but for too long, the
church has not functioned this way.  The teaching of the
word has happened, but only within the walls of a
building.  It's like we have kept the secrets in a box to be
opened and shared only by a chosen few. In addition,
much of the teaching and discipling happened through
the pastor.  That is not the way Jesus intended it.  The
Great Commission (Matthew 28:19-20) was not given to
an institution but rather to individual disciples.  Those
disciples taught others and the kingdom grew. It's called
the Priesthood of all Believers.

In his book, The Present Future, Reggie McNeal notes
"One of the battle cries of the Reformation was Luther's
emphasis on the doctrine of the priesthood of believers."
Reggie McNeal continues that the church has bought into
this concept in a short-sighted and even self-serving
perspective.  "Ministers have waged an enduring
campaign to convince the laity to support the church
efforts with energy, prayer, talent and money."
Unfortunately, this often happens at the expense of being
Jesus in the world.  A lot of money and energy goes into
meeting the church budget so the staff is paid and
facilities are maintained.  Granted, money is set aside for
missions nationally and globally, but little is done to
expand the kingdom locally.  What about grants to
members who want to host events for their neighbors?

---

[44] Ed Stetzer, Subversive Kingdom; Living as Agents of Gospel Transformation, 2012,
Page 28

What about encouraging and supporting house churches that reach people where they are? [45]

I like to think of this ministry model based on Acts 2 as Apostolic Ministry. It begins with training and equipping people to live as missionaries in their neighborhoods.

## Step One: The Apostle's Teaching

It starts with a pastor who supports and encourages people to live as missionaries to their neighborhood. While training and equipping is important, it goes far beyond finding the right manual, buying the right book or even watching a dynamic video series. Missional living is a lifestyle. It permeates from every aspect of the worship on Sunday mornings, to the way leadership meetings are conducted.

The pastor, as the shepherd of the flock, must set the example. The pastor's sermons must not only focus on sound doctrine but also apostolic discipleship. Their lifestyle must also reflect that. That will mean less time in the office and more time being Jesus in the community.

When our son Peter was serving as campus pastor at The Summit in Aledo, Texas, he tried to model this. It helps that for the first few years of their existence they met in a local elementary school. They were forced to hold planning sessions and meetings in alternative sites. Even after they had moved to a permanent worship facility, he continued to hold many meetings at a local Chick-fil-a. I had the opportunity to visit that restaurant once with him. The staff did not treat him like a guest but as a member

---

[45] Reggie McNeal, The Present Future; Six Tough Questions for the Church, Page 45

of the family.  It was obvious that their lives were intertwined.

The term "apostle" is rooted in the Greek language of Jesus' day.  It literally means "one who is sent out."  When I reflect on my years in parish ministry, that is not the model I saw lived out.  The pastor and church staff had offices at the church.  Aside from shut-in visits and hospital calls, I seldom recall my pastor colleague leaving the office.  People came to him when they needed ministry.  As a DCE, I followed the same model.  Aside from occasional home visits, I seldom ventured away from the office.  Part of that was because I was chastised one time for not being "in the office" when someone stopped by to see me.

Following the apostolic model means being Jesus in the world.  In his book, Incarnate: The Body of Christ in an Age of Disengagement, Michael Frost tackles this issue head on.  Early in the book, he states, "I suggest Christianity has become an out-of-body experience – personalized, privatized and customized – and it is being dished out by clergy increasingly disconnected from an incarnational expression of faith." [46]

What I sense Michael Frost is saying is that pastors must model being Jesus in the world and equip and challenge their members to do the same.  The equipping comes through impactful worship that teaches, motivates, and challenges the disciples to be Jesus in the world.  It continues when it is modeled throughout the week.  The teaching, discipling and ministering happens in the world.  A local McDonalds becomes the place where instruction takes place.  A local restaurant becomes the location for one-on-one coaching with a disciple.  The corner

---

[46] Michael Frost, Incarnate, page 31

Starbucks becomes an additional office space where sermons are formed, and Bible classes are prepared.

The Apostles' teachings are always centered on God's Word. The pastor, as the theologian in resident, is responsible for making sure the disciples are trained, and faithful to The Word. When it comes to day-to-day application of God's Word in the lives of the disciples, there has to be a high level of trust.


## Step Two: Fellowship

As I write this, I am sheltered at home because of the 2020 Pandemic. It has been over six months since I was with my brothers and sisters in Christ at church. I long for the opportunity to worship together, probably even more I miss the fellowship we enjoyed. So, while I cannot venture into a crowd, I can still have a "socially distanced" relationship with those around me. The pandemic has given me the opportunity to know my neighbors better. There is Charlie who continues to talk about the need to get back to church but never seems to be able to take the first step. There is Michael who has lost his job and is concerned about finding another one in the midst of an economic downturn. There is Freddie who just enjoys sitting down and sharing a beer together. There are the kids who use the cul-de-sac by our house as their personal playground.

Prior to this point, like most Christians, I had thought of the fellowship in Acts 2:42 as the camaraderie which took place within the "fellowship of believers." I have been challenged to think outside the box, but it is not outside Jesus' box. Or his desire for us. To quote Greg Finke in his book, Joining Jesus on His Mission,  "Jesus enjoyed being with people and knew how to hang out with them." [47]

Jesus did not limit his relationships to those within His circle of friends. Jesus even had a reputation for hanging out with the rejects of society. He admitted it in Matthew 11:19, "The Son of Man came eating and drinking, and they say, 'Here is a glutton and a drunkard, a friend of tax collectors and sinners." (Matthew 11:19)

We are called to be disciples in the world, not hermits behind our privacy fences. There is a whole world of people out there who need to know Jesus' love and grace. The only way that happens is through us.


**Step Three; The Breaking of Bread**

The pandemic also means it has been months since I have been to The Lord's Table. Barb and I have been required to shelter at home. Our only worship is online. Our church had a service of prayer on the eve of the National Day of Prayer. During the opening song, I found myself in tears. My sobbing came from deep inside me. I miss the fellowship with my church family, and oh, how I miss communing with them!

I need the Sacrament of the Altar. I cherish taking the wafer in my hand and contemplating the sacrifice of my Savior that made the gift possible. I know I am receiving His Body, and the forgiveness of sins Jesus earned on my behalf. I yearn to taste the wine, and the renewal that comes through its redeeming power. More than that, I miss the fellowship that I share with my brothers and sisters in Christ as we celebrate the sacrament together.

For a few years, Barb and I were part of The Crossing, a church plant in Dallas. The Crossing was never a large community, peaking at around sixty to seventy

---

[47] Greg Finke, Joining Jesus on His Mission, Page 58

worshippers. There was an intimacy with that community. We worshipped in a high school. We had to work together in setting up and tearing down the worship setting. It became a tight community, with many of us sharing lunch at a local restaurant after worship. We celebrated the Sacrament of the Altar every Sunday. We used a progressive style of distribution with people forming a single line and receiving the elements from the pastor and elders. I often lagged behind, waiting at the end of the line. I suppose some of it was out of courtesy, but I also enjoyed watching people as they stood waiting in anticipation. Being a small flock, I knew the struggles and joys of each of the members. I always marveled at the way God brought us together in that place. I could not help but think I was seeing a glimpse of heaven.

Jesus instituted the Sacrament in the upper room on the night He was betrayed (Matthew 26:17-30). It has always been intriguing to me that the Words of Institution used in our Lutheran liturgy do not come from one of the Gospels but from Paul's first Epistle to the Corinthians (1 Corinthians 11:23-26). The Sacrament was an essential part of who the First Century Christians were and who they worshipped.

This centrality of the Sacrament becomes obvious in the Book of Acts, just after Jesus' Ascension. In his commentary on the Book of Acts, Paul Kretzmann makes it clear the reference to "the breaking of bread'" in Acts 2:42 was not just a reference to a fellowship meal. "It (the breaking of bread) plainly does not refer to an ordinary meal, and was probably used by Luke to describe the common meal which the believers connected with the celebration of the Lord's Supper in the early days of the church." [48]

---

[48] Paul Kretzmann, Popular Commentary of the Bible, New Testament Volume 1, Page 544

Indeed "the breaking of bread" to this day is all about receiving grace and forgiveness, but it is also about celebrating who we are as the Body of Christ. We are a fellowship of broken people who need the love of Jesus. When we celebrate that way, the world will take notice as they did in New Testament time; "Enjoying the favor of all people.". (Acts 2:47) The kingdom cannot help but grow because of it.


## Step Four; Prayers

I turned the corner heading to the house after concluding my afternoon walk. I suddenly realized the sirens I had heard earlier ended up at my neighbors. I was just in time to see them wheel a stretcher carrying my neighbor out the door, with her concerned husband close behind. I inquired what had happened and learned that she had taken a bad fall down the steps. After they had her in the ambulance, I asked my neighbor if I could pray for him and his wife. He nodded and the paramedic motioned I should climb in. Standing in the door of the EMS unit, I prayed a short prayer and they were on their way. As it turned out, there were no broken bones and she was back home later that day. The words of thanks soon followed, as did a conversation about how we can find comfort even in unknown times.

"I will be praying for you." I am worried that it is often a trite expression. Someone shares a concern, medical problem or family issue. We listen and then depart with the promise to pray for them, but how often have I been short on follow through. Working for a hospital chaplaincy services has taught me a valuable lesson. Protocol is that after visiting with a patient I have to wait for them to make the request, "Will you pray for me," before I can offer petitions on their behalf. After ten years of experience, I can sense when the moment is right.  Decorum or not, I am going to initiate the invitation.  I have never been turned down.

Prayer was a key component in the growth of the early church.  They prayed for growth of the kingdom, but they also prayed for each other and those around them.  They were aware of the needs and hurts of those around them.  They showed compassion not only by meeting those needs, but by praying for each other.

Paul was passionate in his prayers for those he held dear.  Consider how many of the Epistles opened with words like:

"I thank my God in all my remembrance of you, always in every prayer of mine for you all making my prayer with joy."  (Philippians 1:3-4)


"We always thank God, the Father of our Lord Jesus Christ, when we pray for you."  (Colossians 1:3)


"We give thanks to God always for all of you, constantly mentioning you in our prayers..." (1 Thessalonians 1:2)


"First of all, then, I urge that supplications, prayers, intercessions and thanksgiving be made for all people." (1 Timothy 2:1)


Prayer is a key component as we seek to build the Kingdom.  We need to not only be praying for our brothers and sisters in Christ, but also for the lost.  The New Testament church "gained favor with all people"

(Acts 2:47a) because of the way they interacted with others.  And it made a difference... "And the Lord added to their number day by day those who were being saved." (Acts 2:47b)

* * * *

Looking to the future, I am encouraged.  The reason for my optimism is found in the promise of Jesus at the time of Peter's confession in Matthew 16: "... and the gates of hell will not overcome it."  Worship communities that are built on the Gospel of Jesus Christ will grow and flourish. Some will be mega churches, other cornerstone churches but more and more of them are going to be like worship communities found in Acts 2.  Some of those communities will be outgrowths of existing churches, but more and more of them are going to be legacy churches; worship communities that come together around the Acts 2 model of teaching, the breaking of bread and prayer.

My prayer is that you will use the following discussion guide.  In four sessions, it will guide you, and those who are part of your worship community, to not only closely examine your current ministry but also look to the future.

"Dear friends, I am not writing you a new command but an old one which you have had since the beginning.  The old command is the message you have heard.  Yet, I am writing a new command, it is truth seen in Him and you, because the darkness is passing, and the true light is already shining."

1 John 2:7-8

# Discussion Guide

# Session 1

# Where Have We Been?

"O God, our help in ages past,

Our hope for years to come,

Our shelter from the stormy blast,

And our eternal home:

(Isaac Watts, 1674-1748)

Discuss your personal history with your church.

How long have you been a member?

What are your favorite memories?

Share a time when the church has particularly impacted your life?

Exodus 12:24-28

The Children of Israel were about to experience the Passover.  They had received very specific instructions on how to prepare that meal.

What further directives does God give in these verses?

Why was this important as they moved forward?

How do these verses speak to the need for us to be mindful of our faith heritage as we move into the future?

2 Timothy 1:3-7

As Paul nears the end of his earthly life, he wanted to provide Timothy with words of encouragement.  Paul reflects on Timothy's spiritual roots.

In verse 6. Paul encourages Timothy to be bold in living out his faith.  What words does he uses?  What are the implications?

In verse 7. Paul encourages Timothy to be bold in his witness.  Reflecting on your spiritual roots, do you think God is calling you and your church to be bold in your walk of discipleship at this time?   How might that happen?

Matthew 5:14-16

How had your church been a light in your community in the past?

How has the church encouraged members to be individual lights?

Is the light of Christ shining through you church as
brightly now as in the past?


Reflect on the words of the hymn found at the beginning
of this session.  What assurance do we have as we not
only reflect on the past but look forward to the future?
Where is that assurance found.

# Session 2

## Where are You Now?

"Built on the Rock the Church shall stand,

Even when steeples are falling;

Crumbled have spires in every land,

Bells still are chiming and calling,

Calling the young and old to rest,

Calling the souls of those distressed,

Longing for life everlasting."

Discuss what you see in your church right now?  What are you doing well?  What could you be doing better?

How does your church compare to what it was five years or ten years ago?  Do not just consider membership and church attendance.  Consider the age and level of activity of the membership.  How many new members have joined the congregation?

How do the words to the hymn above, provide you with hope as consider your church and its ministry?

Joshua 4:1-7


The Children of Israel had crossed the Jordan and
arrived in the promise land.


How did Joshua instruct them to commemorate the
event?


As you look around your church building, what objects
do you see that commemorate your congregation's
heritage?


How do those items help your church stay focused on the
ministry your worship community has today?

1 Timothy 2:1-7


What is Paul telling Timothy about worship?


What does Paul see as one of the most important goals of
worship? (vs 4)


How should this be played out in the way we view and
use our worship facilities?


John 2:12-23

How do you think Jesus would react if He visited you
church facilities?  What do the facilities say about your
ministry and how people are equipped to be disciples?


How should this challenge us to rethink how we currently
do ministry?

# Session 3

# Where are We Going?

Guide me O Thou great Jehovah,

Pilgrim through this barren land.

I am weak, but you are mighty,

Hold me with thy powerful hand,

Bread of heaven, bread of heaven,

Feed me now and evermore; Feed me now and
evermore.

This book suggests a number of potential changes regarding the future of churches in America from the decline of mainline denominations to the devaluing of church building.

Select one or two of those changes and discuss what the implications might be for your church?

In anticipation of those changes, what adjustments might your congregation need to make in the way that you do ministry?

Comparisons have been made between the situation Daniel and the other exiles faced in Babylon and the circumstances Christians find themselves in today.  Some have even labeled our current culture as a "digital Babylon."  Consider that as you read the following Old Testament passages.

Daniel 1: 1-21

What was Daniel's response to the orders of King Nebuchadnezzar?  How did God bless Daniel and his friends?

Jeremiah 29: 4-14

What were God's instructions to the exiles living Babylon?  How might those instructions apply to us today?

What words of hope are found in verse 11?   How might that encourage you as a church leader today?

John 6:60-71

Jesus had some challenging words to say to His disciples in terms of their walk of discipleship.  How do they apply to us today?

How did His disciples respond when asked whether they wanted to "leave" to?


What was significant about Peter's words? (vs 68)


How do might these words apply to us as we face a challenging time when the culture has changed?

# Session 4

# How are You Going to Get There?

God of grace and God of Glory,

On your people pour your power,

Crown your ancient church's story,

Bring its bud to glorious flower,

Grant us wisdom, grant us courage,

For the facing of this hour,

For the facing of this hour.

Thus far we have looked at the past history of your church and then compared that to where you are now.  In the last session we discussed what the future might possibly look like.  Now the real challenge, how are you going to get there?

As the above hymn reminds us, the church has a glorious history going back thousands of years.  Past leaders have sought God's guidance as they navigated the culture of their day.  Now God is calling us to do the same.  God is indeed faithful and he will guide us as we face this "trying" hour.

Joshua 24:1-27

Joshua had served as leader of the Children of Israel following the death of Moses. He had led them into the Promised Land but now his time was drawing to a close. What message did Joshua have for the people? What did that require of them? Joshua made his own statement of commitment in verse 15b. Why was it important for the people to hear that? How will be the members of your church hear that message from you as one of the leaders?

John 21:13-19

What was Jesus calling Peter to do that this point? Considering Peter's recent past history with Jesus (see John 18, 15-18 & 25-27) why was this important? Why is it important for you to personally to hear Jesus' question, "_____ do you love me?" How will your response impact the future of your personal walk of discipleship? How might it effect the long-term ministry of your church?

Acts 2:42-47

Consider the outline for growing the Kingdom of God in vs. 42. How will that be lived out in your local congregation in the future? What changes do you anticipate?

# Meet the Author

Tom Couser has over fifty years of experience in ministry.  He served over twenty-five years as a director of Christian education (DCE) and an addition eleven years as a high school counselor.  In retirement he continues to work as a writer/consultant helping churches adapt to the changing culture.  Two of his previous books, Passing the Torch and Relevant, explored how the church can better reach out to Millennials. Tom publishes a weekly Passing the Torch newsletter that focuses on current topics of interest. Tom and his wife, Barb, live in Dallas, Texas. In addition to their sons Peter and Mark, who you met through this book, their daughter, Katie Seale, serves as director of worship at Prince of Peace Lutheran Church in Carrollton, Texas.  They are proud to have four grandsons and one precious granddaughter.  You can contact him as thomascouser@yahoo.com.

www.ingramcontent.com/pod-product-compliance
Lightning Source LLC
Chambersburg PA
CBHW052109150726
48002CB00006B/2287